POSTCARDS 2

Language Booster

Workbook
with Grammar Builder

Brian Abbs
Chris Barker
Ingrid Freebairn

LONGMAN ON THE **WEB**

Longman.com offers online resources for teachers
and students. Access our Companion Websites, our
online catalog, and our local offices around the world.

Longman English Success offers online courses
to give learners flexible study options. Courses cover
General English, Business English, and Exam Preparation.

Visit us at **longman.com** and **englishsuccess.com**.

longman.com

Postcards 2 Language Booster

Pearson Education, 10 Bank Street, White Plains, NY 10606

Vice president, director of publishing: Allen Ascher
Editorial director: Ed Lamprich
Publisher: Sherri Arbogast
Senior development editors: Jose Antonio Mendez, Marilyn Hochman
Development editor: Tunde Dewey
Vice president, director of design and production: Rhea Banker
Executive managing editor: Linda Moser
Production manager: Liza Pleva
Associate managing editor: Mike Kemper
Associate production editor: Michael Goldberg
Director of manufacturing: Patrice Fraccio
Senior manufacturing buyer: Dave Dickey
Photo research: Aerin Csigay
Cover design: Ann France
Text design: Ann France and Pearson Education Development Group
Text composition: Circa 86 and Pearson Education Development Group
Text font: 11/14 palatino

ISBN: 0-13-093902-1

Printed in the United States of America

10 9 8 7 6 5 – PBP – 07 06 05

The authors and publisher wish to acknowledge the contribution of **David McKeegan** for writing the activities in the Workbook.

Illustration credits

pp. 17, 35, 44 Dave Carleson; pp. 28, 107 Dave Coulson; p.73 Renee Daily; pp. 31, 34, 44, 69 Daniel DelValle; p.97 John Faulkner; pp. 18, 83 Adam Gordon; p.12 Peter Gunther; p.111 George Hamblin; pp. 22, 34, 46, 52, 68, 75, 97, 98 Michael Hortens; pp. 23, 32, 41 Laura Hartman Maestro; p.102, Dan Martinetti; P.35, Stephanie Pershing; p.106 Dusan Petricic (left and right), Pierre Berthiaume (center); pp. 55, 87, 105 Barbara Pollak; pp. 14, 105, 107 Chris Reed; pp. 15, 19, 49, 88, 102 Bart Rivers; pp. 18, 31, 90 Lauren Scheuer; p.38 Andrew Shiff; p.39, Karen Stevens; p.9 Dan Tesser; pp. 37, 56, 65, 90, 94, 101, 103, 109, 110 George Thompson; p. 27 Anna Veltfort; p.81 Deborah White; p.98 John Wisniewski (Wiz); pp. 9, 13, 27, 70, 81, 89, 92 Ron Zalme

Photo credits

p.18 Michael Krasowitz/Getty Images/Taxi; p.21 PhotoDisc, Inc.; p.23 AWL/Trevor Clifford; p.24 Jose Luis Pelaez, Inc./Corbis, Ed Bock Photography, Inc./Corbis, Ariel Skelley/Corbis; p.31 Stephen Ogilvey; p.39 AFP/Corbis; p.53 AWL/Trevor Clifford; p.58 Superstock; 66 Will & Deni McIntyre/Getty Images/Stone; p.78 PhotoDisc, Inc.; p.79 Jon Bradley/Getty Images/Stone.

Welcome to the Language Booster!

This book will give you lots of practice in grammar, vocabulary, and communication skills.

The Workbook

The Language Booster begins with a Workbook section (pages 8–61). It's a workbook with a difference—the exercises in each category (Grammar, Vocabulary, and Communication) are separated into three levels: Getting Started (easy), Moving Up (harder), and Reaching for the Top (challenging). You and your teacher can choose the level that suits you best, or you can work through all the exercises if you like. When you feel confident with one level, you can move on to the next.

After every four units in the Workbook section, there's a Skills Development lesson with an engaging reading. Following the reading are vocabulary, comprehension, and writing activities. In the first reading, you'll read about three American teenagers and how they spend their pocket money. In the second reading, you'll read about a strange experience at the Palace of Versailles, France, in 1901. And in the third reading, you'll read about one family's emigration frm Ireland to America in 1854.

The Grammar Builder

The second part of the Language Booster is called the Grammar Builder (pages 63–111), and it contains additional grammar exercises. It also includes grammar reference sections called Grammar Highlights so that you can check on grammar rules while you are doing the exercises. You can work through the units in the Grammar Builder simultaneously with the units in the Workbook section, or you can do them at a later stage.

We hope that this Language Booster, with its special features, will give you all the help you need to learn English successfully–and enjoyably.

Scope and Sequence

Grammar Builder

Scope and Sequence

Workbook

Grammar Builder

Communication	Pages	Grammar

• Talk about past events
• Agree or disagree with someone
	88–91	• Simple past: regular verbs
		  – Affirmative and negative statements
		  – *Yes/No* questions
		  – Information questions

• Talk about past events • Express opinions	**92–95**	• Simple past: irregular verbs • Coordinate conjunctions: *and*, *but*, *so*
• Narrate a past event • Talk about the weather	**96–99**	• The past continuous with *when* and *while* • Simple past contrasted with past continuous
• Ask and express preferences or choices *(Which)*	**100–103**	• Comparative and superlative forms of adjectives • *As* + adjective + *as*
• Give advice	**104–107**	• *Should/Shouldn't* • Habitual past: *used to*

• Express possibility with *may* and *might*	**108–111**	• Simple future: *will*
		  – Affirmative and negative statements
		  – *Yes/No* questions
		• *May* and *might*

1 We're members of Teen Scenes.

Grammar

Getting Started

1 Read Koko's e-mail. Circle the correct form of the verb *be*.

Hi, Julia,

It (**1.** (**'s**)/ *'m*) me, Koko. How (**2.** *is* / *are*) you? I (**3.** *'s* / *'m*) fine. I (**4.** *'m not* / *'re not*) at school at the moment because my parents and I (**5.** *am* / *are*) on vacation. Guess what? I have a new boyfriend. His name (**6.** *is* / *am*) Felix. He (**7.** *is* / *am*) tall and handsome. He (**8.** *isn't* / *aren't*) from around here. He and his parents (**9.** *is* / *are*) Brazilian. I met his parents last week, and they (**10.** *'s* / *'re*) really cool. Write soon and tell me your news!

Best,
Koko

Moving Up

2 Complete the questions. Then write short answers.

1. __Is__ Koko at school?
   No, she isn't.

2. _____ Koko and her parents on vacation?
   _____

3. _____ Koko's boyfriend short?
   _____

4. _____ Koko's boyfriend's name Oscar?
   _____

5. _____ Felix's parents American?
   _____

6. _____ Felix's parents from Brazil?
   _____

3 Read the answers. Then complete the information questions with *Who, Where, When,* or *What.*

1. A: ___What___ are those under the table?
   B: Those are my dirty sneakers.
2. A: _____ is the party?
   B: It's next Sunday.
3. A: _____ are your parents?
   B: They're on vacation.
4. A: _____ is your next class?
   B: It's English.
5. A: _____ is your English teacher?
   B: Mrs. Scott.

4 Complete the conversations with possessive pronouns. Write *mine, yours, his, hers, theirs,* or *ours.*

1. A: Excuse me. Is this puppy ___yours___?

   B: No, it isn't _____. I think it's

   _____.

2. A: Excuse me. Is this puppy _____?

   B: No. I think it's _____.

3. A: Excuse me. Is this puppy yours?

   B: No, it isn't. Do you see those people over there? I think it's _____.

4. A: Well, it isn't theirs.

   B: OK, we can keep it. It's _____ now!

   A: Hooray!

Reaching for the Top

5 Circle the correct words.

1. Whose cassette player is this?
   Is it (*your* / *yours*)?

2. I can't find (*my* / *mine*) computer magazines.

3. Luis is doing his homework, but Carmen isn't doing (*her* / *hers*).

4. Did you pass (*your* / *yours*) exams this year?

5. That green backpack is (*my* / *mine*).

6. (*Our* / *Ours*) basketball team is good, but (*their* / *theirs*) isn't good at all.

7. I love (*her* / *hers*) house! It's much nicer than (*our* / *ours*).

Vocabulary

Getting Started

6 Circle ten adjectives that describe people and their hair. The words go down, across, and diagonally.

```
O  R  N  E  R  E  M  O  F  S
C  O  S  M  A  R  T  Y  R  H
C  U  T  P  R  H  I  T  I  A
B  W  R  E  F  O  I  R  E  N
L  O  A  L  A  U  N  I  N  D
O  L  I  V  Y  S  N  G  D  S
N  A  G  R  Y  O  O  N  L  O
D  M  H  P  R  E  T  T  Y  M
A  S  T  R  O  N  G  I  N  E
```

Moving Up

7 Write the adjectives from Exercise 6 in the correct columns.

Hair	Physical appearance	Personality
wavy		

8 Look at the pictures. Then complete the name of each object. Write the missing letters.

1. c a s s e t t e p l a y e r
2. C __ __ __ __ y __ r
3. __ a __ __ z __ __ __ __
4. v __ __ __ __ g __ __ __
5. __ o __ __ __ b __ __ __ __
6. __ __ __ k __ __ __ k
7. c __ __ __ __ __ __ __ r __ __ __ n __
8. __ __ __ __ __ r b __ __ __

Reaching for the Top

9 Complete the clues. Then write the words in the puzzle.

Across

1. Her hair isn't curly or wavy. It's _straight_.
4. *Shrek* was a very _____ movie. It made us laugh.
8. I bought a fashion _____ to read on the train.
9. Paco is very _____. He can lift that heavy box for you.

Down

1. Another word for *clever* is _____.
2. A boy who is good-looking is _____.
3. I carry my books and notebooks in my _____.
5. It's not funny. It's _____.
6. A _____ book is full of picture stories.
7. She loves to play that _____ on her new computer.

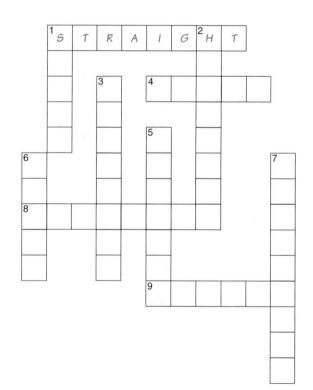

Communication

Getting Started

10 Complete the conversation with the questions from the box.

Really? What's her name?
Hey, can you introduce us, please?
~~Hey, Gus. How are you doing?~~
And how old is she?
Is she pretty?

Foster: (1) *Hey, Gus. How are you doing?*

Gus: I'm fine, thanks. Guess what? There's a new girl in my class.

Foster: (2) _____

_____

Gus: Elizabeth.

Foster: (3) _____

_____

Gus: Oh, yes. She's very pretty. She's of average height and thin.

Foster: (4) _____

_____

Gus: She's fifteen.

Foster: (5) _____

_____

Reaching for the Top

11 Imagine that a new boy (or girl) has arrived in your class. Write an imaginary conversation between you and a friend about the new classmate. Use the conversation in Exercise 10 as a model.

_____

_____

_____

_____

_____

_____

_____

_____

_____

_____

_____

_____

_____

_____

2 Let's make pizza.

Vocabulary

Getting Started

1 What does Julia do when she gets home from school? Look at the pictures. Then put the phrases in the correct order. Write the numbers.

_____ listens to music

_____ chats on the Internet

__1__ has a snack

_____ does her homework

_____ watches TV

2 Write sentences about Julia's routine. Use each sequence word only once: *First, Next, Then, After that,* and *Finally.*

1. *First, she has a snack.* _____

2. _____

3. _____

4. _____

5. _____

Moving Up

3 Unscramble the words to write the names of some cooking ingredients. Then match each food item with the correct picture. Write the letter of the picture next to the item.

1. t r e t u b   ___butter___   _e_

2. m a o t t s o e _____ ____

3. s e h e c e   _____ ____

4. r u a g s   _____ ____

5. s g e g   _____ ____

6. s p o e a t o t _____ ____

7. n o i n o s   _____ ____

a.

b.

c.

d.

e.

f.

g.

Reaching for the Top

4 Complete the sentences with the words from the box.

cheese	tomato	pepper	omelette
onion	eggs	oil	milk

1. To make an omelette, first break two _eggs_ into a cup.

2. Add some _____ to the eggs to make them lighter. Beat the egg mixture.

3. Chop up a _____ and add it to the egg mixture.

4. Then put some _____ in a pan. Heat up the pan.

5. Chop an _____ into small pieces and fry it until it is soft.

6. Pour the egg mixture into the pan with the onions. Add some salt and _____.

7. Before the egg becomes hard, put some _____ on it. Let the cheese melt.

8. Now fold the _____, put it on a plate, and eat it!

Grammar

Getting Started

5 Read the sentences and circle the nouns. Then write *SC* next to the singular count nouns, *PC* next to the plural count nouns, and *NC* next to the noncount nouns.

1. We love those (cookies)   _PC_

2. She loves tomatoes.   _____

3. Give me an egg, please.   _____

4. Where did you put the rice?   _____

5. There's some milk over there.   _____

6. Do we have any onions?   _____

7. Put them in the pan.   _____

8. I need some water.   _____

9. Can I have some butter?   _____

10. I'd like some ice cream.   _____

Moving Up

6 Look at the picture. Then complete each sentence. Circle the letter next to the correct answer.

1. _____ potatoes in the refrigerator.

(a.) There aren't any   b. There are some   c. There is a

2. _____ egg.

a. There isn't any   b. There is some   c. There is an

3. _____ milk.

a. There isn't any   b. There is some   c. There is a

4. _____ tomatoes.

a. There are some   b. There is some   c. There is a

5. _____ water.

a. There isn't any   b. There are some   c. There is a

6. _____ cheese.

a. There aren't any   b. There is some   c. There is a

7. _____ hot dogs.

a. There aren't any   b. There are some   c. There is some

Reaching for the Top

7 Write questions about the picture in Exercise 6. Use the cues.

1. (rice) _Is there any/some rice?_____
2. (milk) _____
3. (cheese) _____
4. (tomatoes) _____
5. (butter) _____
6. (onions) _____
7. (egg) _____
8. (lemonade) _____
9. (hot dogs) _____
10. (dough) _____

8 Write answers to the questions in Exercise 7. Use contractions when possible.

1. _No, there isn't._____
2. _____
3. _____
4. _____
5. _____
6. _____
7. _____
8. _____
9. _____
10. _____

Communication

Moving Up

9 Put the lines of the conversation in the correct order. Write the numbers. Then write the conversation in the correct order on the lines.

_____ Let's see . . . Yes, there's some cheese in here, too. Do we have any oil?

_____ Me, too. Hey, let's make an omelette!

_____ Oh, no! I just remembered. We don't have any eggs!

_____ Yes, there are some tomatoes in the refrigerator.

__1__ Gee, I'm so hungry.

_____ OK, sure. Uh . . . , do we have any tomatoes?

_____ I think so. Yes, there's some oil in the cabinet.

_____ What about cheese?

_____ In the cabinet? Good. I'll put some oil in the pan, and you break some eggs.

Gee, I'm so hungry. _____

_____

_____

_____

(right column blank lines)

Reaching for the Top

10 In your notebook, write a conversation between you and a friend about preparing something good to eat. Use the conversation in Exercise 9 as a model.

How much do we need?

Vocabulary

Getting Started

1 Look at the pictures. Then complete the names of the food items. Write the missing letters.

1. c _e_ _r_ _e_ _a_ l
2. y _ _ r _
3. _ i _ _
4. _ o o _ _ _
5. b _ _ _ _
6. _ _ _ p _ s
7. _ a _ _ a
8. _ h _ _ _ n
9. _ r _ _ _
10. _ _ _ t t _ _ _
11. _ _ r r _ _
12. _ a _
13. _ t _ _ _ _ _ r r _
14. _ a _ a _ a
15. _ i _ _

Moving Up

2 Write the words from Exercise 1 in the puzzle. Which item does not fit? Write it on the line. _____

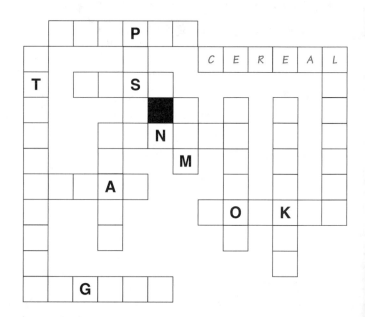

Reaching for the Top

3 Write the words from Exercise 1 in the correct columns.

Count nouns	Noncount nouns
cookie	cereal
_____	_____
_____	_____
_____	_____
_____	_____
_____	_____
	_____
	_____
	_____

Grammar

Getting Started

4 Complete the sentences. Circle **how much** or **how many**.

Interviewer: Today, I'm talking to athlete Rosa Blanco. Rosa, (1. *how much* / *how many*) time do you spend training every day?

Rosa: I train for two hours in the morning and three hours in the evening.

Interviewer: Wow! That's a lot. (2. *How much* / *How many*) days a week do you train?

Rosa: Every day.

Interviewer: You must get very tired! (3. *How much* / *How many*) hours do you sleep at night?

Rosa: I try to get at least eight hours of sleep every night.

Interviewer: What about your diet? (4. *How much* / *How many*) fruit do you eat every day?

Rosa: I eat a lot of fruit. Especially oranges. I love oranges.

Interviewer: (5. *How much* / *How many*) oranges do you eat in a day?

Rosa: Oh, usually three. Sometimes five!

Interviewer: What about junk food? (6. *How much* / *How many*) junk food do you eat?

Rosa: I never eat junk food!

talk

Moving Up

5 Look at Marco's shopping list. Then read the answers and write the questions.

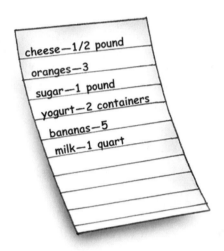

cheese—1/2 pound
oranges—3
sugar—1 pound
yogurt—2 containers
bananas—5
milk—1 quart

1. *How much yogurt did he buy?*

   Two containers.

2. _____

   Half a pound.

3. _____

   Five.

4. _____

   One pound.

5. _____

   Three.

6. _____

   One quart.

6 Read the questions. Then write your answers using *a little* or *a few*.

1. How much chocolate did you eat last night?
   A little.

2. How many cookies did you eat at the party?

   _____

3. How much money do you have?

   _____

4. How many friends do you have?

   _____

5. How much milk is there in your refrigerator?

   _____

Reaching for the Top

7 Complete the sentences. Write *a little, a few,* or *a lot of* and one of the words from the box.

Japanese	houses	salt	days
strength	~~money~~	water	

1. I can't go out for dinner tonight because I don't have *a lot of money* _____.

2. Don't forget to put _____ in the soup—but not too much!

3. Today is June 19—only _____ left before classes end.

4. It was very hot yesterday, so I drank _____.

5. I live in a very small town. There are only _____ in it.

6. I understand some of what Masako says because I speak _____.

7. You need _____ to lift 50 pounds!

Communication

Getting Started

8 Complete the conversation with the sentences from the box.

> Oh, that's too much. I'll just have the strawberries and the bread, please.
> Yes. How much is the bread?
> Thank you. Bye.
> I'll have two boxes, please.
> I'll have a loaf, please. And how much are the grapes?
> ~~Yes, please. How much are the strawberries?~~

1. A: Can I help you?
   B: *Yes, please. How much are the*
      strawberries?

2. A: The strawberries are $2.00 for a small box.
   B: _____

3. A: That's $4.00. Anything else?
   B: _____

4. A: It's $1.50 for a loaf.
   B: _____
      _____

5. A: They're $5.00 a bunch.
   B: _____
      _____

6. A: That's $5.50 altogether.
   B: _____

Moving Up

9 Number the lines of the conversation in the correct order. Then write the conversation in the correct order on the lines below.

_____ I bought a loaf.

_____ I bought some strawberries.

_____ One loaf is enough for today. Great.

_____ Good. And what about bread? How much bread did you buy?

_____ How many boxes of strawberries did you buy?

_1_ What did you buy at the grocery store, Mark?

_____ Two boxes.

_____
_____
_____
_____
_____
_____
_____
_____
_____
_____
_____

Reaching for the Top

10 Imagine that you are buying food for your family. Write a conversation between you and the grocer. Use the conversation in Exercise 8 as a model.

Can I help you?
_____
_____
_____
_____
_____
_____
_____
_____
_____

How often do you skate?

Vocabulary

Getting Started

1 Look at the pictures. Then write the name of each sport or leisure activity in the puzzle. Use a dictionary if you need help.

1.
2.
3.
4.
5.
6.
7.
8.
9.
10.

1. S K I I N G
2.
3.
4.
5.
6.
7.
8.
9.
10.

2 What is the mystery sport? Write it on the line. _____

Moving Up

3 Write the sport and leisure activities from Exercise 1 in the correct columns.

Sports on wheels	Sports with balls	Water sports	Other sports
biking	volleyball		

Reaching for the Top

4 Read the sentences. Then write the names of the sports.

1. You play this game with a ball. You hit the ball over a net with your hands. You can play this game on the beach. ___volleyball___

2. This game is very popular in the United States. There are nine people on each team. You hit the ball with a bat and run around three bases to reach home. _____

3. You do this sport on the water. You stand on a board with a sail. The wind on the sail moves the board along the surface of the water. _____

4. You wear boots with wheels on the bottom to do this sport. You can go very fast, but try not to fall down! _____

5. In this sport, there are 11 players on each team. Only the goalkeeper may touch the ball with his or her hands. _____

6. In this sport, there are 5 players on each team. This ball game is easier if you are very tall. _____

Grammar

Getting Started

5 Complete the sentences with the gerund (-*ing* form) of the verbs in parentheses.

My name is Monica Gibbons, and I like (*play*) ___playing___ all kinds of sports. I
(1)
especially like (*swim*) _____ and other
(2)
water sports. Windsurfing is very exciting, but I only do that in the summer. Athletics is fun, too, and I really enjoy (*run*) _____. Ball
(3)
games are fantastic! I like (*play*) _____
(4)
volleyball and soccer with my friends on the beach. There are only a few sports I don't like. I'm afraid of heights, so I don't enjoy (*climb*)
_____. I also hate (*skate*) _____
(5)   (6)
anywhere!

Moving Up

6 What kinds of sports do you like? Write true sentences about yourself using the cues.

Examples: _I like biking._

I hate running.

1. (*like*) _____
2. (*hate*) _____
3. (*enjoy*) _____
4. (*go*) _____
5. (*love*) _____
6. (*finish*) _____

7 How often does Marta do her favorite activities? Look at the chart. Then write questions and answers using adverbs of frequency.

Activities	Monday	Tuesday	Wednesday	Thursday	Friday	Saturday	Sunday
1. go out for a hamburger			✓			✓	
2. play basketball							
3. wash her hair	✓		✓		✓		
4. call her boyfriend	✓	✓	✓	✓	✓	✓	✓
5. go to the movies						✓	

1. *How often does she go out for a hamburger?*
   Twice a week.

2. _____
   _____

3. _____
   _____

4. _____
   _____

5. _____
   _____

Reaching for the Top

8 How often do you do these sports and activities? Write four sentences. For each sentence, use an activity or sport from the first box and an adverb or phrase of frequency from the second box.

Activities and sports	Adverbs and phrases of frequency
• go to the movies • watch TV • buy a magazine • wash your hair • play soccer • go to school • do your homework • buy candy • visit your grandparents (or other relatives)	• every day (week, month, year) • never • once (twice, three times) a week • once (twice, three times) a month • once (twice, three times) a year

1. *I go to the movies once a week.*

2. _____

3. _____

4. _____

5. _____

Communication

Getting Started

9 Complete the conversation. Use *can*, *can't*, or the gerund form of a verb.

Katy: _____Can_____ you skate, Rico?
(1)

Rico: Yes, I _____. Everyone in my family
(2)

_____ skate. We like _____ a lot.
(3)   (4)

Katy: I _____ skate. But I like _____
(5)   (6)

it on TV.

Rico: _____ your brother skate?
(7)

Katy: No, he _____. He hates _____.
(8)   (9)

Rico: But he _____ ski, right?
(10)

Katy: No, he _____.
(11)

Rico: Are you sure?

Katy: I'm quite sure. He hates _____! In
(12)

fact, he hates all sports. He's a real

couch potato!

Moving Up

10 Complete the conversation. Write the questions.

Cora: (1) *Can you windsurf?* _____

Lucas: No, I can't.

Cora: (2) _____

Lucas: Yes, I can. I love skiing.

Cora: (3) _____

Lucas: Yes, I can skate, too.

Cora: (4) _____

Lucas: I go skating twice a week. There's a skating rink near my house.

Cora: (5) _____

Lucas: Of course, I can teach you to skate! It's easy!

Reaching for the Top

11 In your notebook, write a conversation between you and a friend about favorite sports. Use Exercise 10 as a model.

Study Corner

Increase your verb power
When you are learning new verbs, make special notes about the verbs that have spelling changes. Use a chart like the one below.

Base form of verb	Third-person singular/ simple present tense	Gerund (*-ing* form)
go	goes	going
run	runs	running
have	has	having

12 Add these verbs to your study corner chart.

come   put   do   write   live   win

Reading

SPENDING
American teenagers speak out about their money
POWER

▶ **Alana Davies, 15**

I get an allowance of $15 every week from my parents. I also have some birthday money and some savings in the bank. I'm saving up money for a CD player. I spend my money on clothes, movie tickets, and candy. I like to be in good physical shape, so I often work out in the gym. I pay for my gym membership every month. On weekends, I visit with friends and go skateboarding.

▶ **Jose Molina, 14**

Every week, I get an allowance of $10 from my parents. I'm trying to get a part-time job selling CDs at a music store. I usually spend my money on CDs, computer games, and movie tickets. On Friday and Saturday evenings, I usually go out with my friends to the movies or to parties.

▶ **Kathy Bethell, 17**

I get an allowance of $20 a week from my parents. I also baby-sit and make another $20 every week from that job. I'm putting aside money for my summer vacation. I spend my money on clothes, magazines, and on going out to dance clubs and the movies. I love dancing and going to the movies.

Vocabulary

1 Find the words below in the reading. Then circle the letter next to the correct definition for each word.

1. allowance
   a. food
   b. money to spend
   c. free time

2. part-time job
   a. work done for a few hours a week
   b. work done for no pay
   c. work done very fast

3. savings
   a. expressions
   b. coins
   c. money saved

4. be in good physical shape
   a. have a strong body
   b. be lucky
   c. look fashionable

5. baby-sit
   a. sit like a baby
   b. take care of somebody's child
   c. make children sit

6. make $20.00
   a. put $20.00 in the bank
   b. print $20.00
   c. get $20.00 for work you do

7. put aside
   a. borrow something
   b. save something
   c. turn to the side

Comprehension

2 Fill in the chart. Write the information about Alana and Kathy.

	Jose (14)	Alana (15)	Kathy (17)
Spending money • allowance • job	$10 a week no job		
Spends money on:	clothes CDs computer games movie tickets		
Social life:	goes to movies and parties		

3 Complete the sentences. Write the names of the people from the reading.

1. _Kathy_ has a part-time job.
2. _____ is a member of a gym.
3. _____ is trying to get a job.
4. _____ are saving money for different things.
5. _____ has some money in the bank.
6. _____ like going to the movies.
7. _____ likes candy.
8. _____ receives the most money each week.

Writing

4 In your notebook, write a paragraph about how you get money and how you spend it. Include the following information in your paragraph:

- how much money you get every week/month
- who or where you get the money from
- how much money you save
- what you spend your money on
- how much you spend on your social life
- what you like to do

5 He's reading.

Grammar

Getting Started

1 Read the paragraph and look at the picture. Then complete the sentences with the present continuous form of the verbs. Use contractions when possible.

Keiko Kenji Matt Rosa Billy Susan

I'm Susan. Today is my birthday. My friends and I are having a party. We're in the backyard of my house. We're having lots of fun. The weather is wonderful.

1. Rosa and Matt (*play*) _are playing_ volleyball.

2. Billy (*listen*) _____ to music.

3. Keiko and Kenji (*swim*) _____ in the pool.

4. The kids (*not/take*) _____ photographs.

5. The dog (*sleep*) _____ under the table.

6. It (*not/rain*) _____ today.

7. Susan (*eat*) _____ a hot dog.

2 Write questions and short answers. Use the cues and the picture.

1. Rosa and Matt / sit

   Are Rosa and Matt sitting?

   No, they aren't.

2. Susan / read a book

   _____

   _____

3. the kids / have a birthday party

   _____

   _____

4. Billy / listen to music

   _____

   _____

5. the dog / run

   _____

   _____

6. Keiko and Kenji / dance

   _____

   _____

7. the kids / have fun

   _____

   _____

Moving Up

3 **Look at the picture in Exercise 1. Read the answers. Then write questions using *Where*, *Who*, *What*, or *Why* and the present continuous form of an appropriate verb.**

1. *Where are the kids having the party?*

   In Susan's backyard.

2. _____

   Billy is listening to music.

3. _____

   Susan is having a birthday party.

4. _____

   Keiko and Kenji are swimming.

5. _____

   In the pool.

6. _____

   Because it is Susan's birthday.

7. _____

   A hot dog.

8. _____

   Under the table.

Reaching for the Top

4 **Circle the correct answer in each conversation.**

1. A: What (*are you looking for* / *do you look for*) under the bed?

   B: (*I'm looking for* / *I look for*) my sneakers.

2. A: What (*are you usually doing* / *do you usually do*) after school?

   B: Well, (*I'm usually hanging out* / *I usually hang out*) with my friends.

3. A: Look! (*It's raining.* / *It rains.*)

   B: That's strange. (*It never rains* / *It's never raining*) here in August.

4. A: What (*are you doing* / *do you do*) right now?

   B: (*I'm playing* / *I play*) video games.

5. A: (*I'm making* / *I make*) my lunch every morning.

   B: Really? (*I'm never having* / *I never have*) that much time in the morning.

6. A: Where's Tony? (*Is he playing* / *Does he play*) tennis again?

   B: I think so. He (*is playing* / *plays*) tennis every Saturday.

7. A: Why (*are we usually having* / *do we usually have*) a lot of homework?

   B: It's a lot, but it's easy. I (*am doing* / *do*) mine right now!

8. A: Who (*is making* / *makes*) noise? I can't study.

   B: I think Sam (*is playing* / *plays*) his guitar.

Vocabulary

Getting Started

5 Find the hobbies. Match the words from Column A with the words from Column B to make phrases. Write the letters.

	A	B
_f_	1. playing	a. pictures
___	2. reading	b. TV
___	3. drawing	c. coins
___	4. flying	d. books
___	5. watching	e. photographs
___	6. taking	f. board games
___	7. collecting	g. museums
___	8. visiting	h. a kite

Moving Up

6 Complete the sentences with the phrases from Exercise 5.

1. We're _playing board games_ because it's raining.

2. My older brother is _____ in his room. I think he's watching a soccer game.

3. My dad is _____ with his digital camera.

4. I enjoy _____, especially natural history museums.

5. My sister enjoys _____. She especially likes mysteries.

6. Look at these sketches! He's really good at _____.

7. Emily's hobby is _____. She has money from many countries.

8. Ana is _____ at the beach.

Reaching for the Top

7 Look at the pictures. Then write what the people are doing. Use contractions.

1. _He's taking photographs._ _____

2. _____

3. _____

4. _____

Communication

Moving Up

8 Complete the conversation. Use the present continuous or the simple present form of the verbs in parentheses. Use contractions when possible.

Mateo: Hi, Jessica. It's Mateo. What
(*you / do*) ___are you doing___ ?
(1)

Jessica: I (*prepare*) _____
(2)
dinner for my family.

Mateo: Dinner? It's only five o'clock. (*you /
usually cook*) _____
(3)
this early?

Jessica: No, not usually. Mom (*usually / cook*)
_____, but she
(4)
(*not / feel*) _____
(5)
well right now.

Mateo: I'm sorry to hear that. Listen, I (*plan*)
_____ to go to the
(6)
movies tonight. (*you / want*)
_____ to come?
(7)

Jessica: No, thanks. I (*never / go*)
_____ out on
(8)
Thursdays.

Mateo: Well, maybe tomorrow then?

Jessica: OK. Look, I have to go now. Mom
(*call*) _____ me.
(9)

Mateo: OK. See you tomorrow.

Jessica: Bye.

Reaching for the Top

9 Go to a park, a supermarket, or another busy place. In your notebook, write eight sentences about the things you see people doing.

Example: _Children are running around in the park._

6 What are you going to wear?

Vocabulary

Getting Started

1 Look at the pictures. Write the words from the box under the correct pictures.

~~boots~~	hat	sandals	sneakers	T-shirt
cap	jacket	scarf	socks	tights
coat	jeans	shoes	sweater	top
dress	pants	skirt	sweatshirt	windbreaker
gloves				

1. _boots_

2. _____

3. _____

4. _____

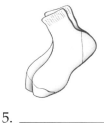
5. _____

6. _____

7. _____

8. _____

9. _____

10. _____

11. _____

12. _____

13. _____

14. _____

15. _____

16. _____

17. _____

18. _____

19. _____

20. _____

21. _____

Reaching for the Top

2 Look at the pictures. Write what each person is wearing.

1. Scott is wearing *a scarf, a jacket, a sweater, gloves, pants, socks, and shoes* _____ .

2. Melissa is wearing _____ .

3. Bruce is wearing _____ .

4. Terry is wearing _____ .

Grammar

Getting Started

3 Complete Monica's e-mail. Write the correct form of *be going to* and the verb in parentheses. Use contractions when possible.

Hi, Maria,

Guess what? My mom and I *(go)* ___*are going to go*___ to Hong Kong on vacation
                   (1)

tomorrow! I'm really excited. My dad *(drive)* _____ us to the airport in
                  (2)

the morning, and we *(leave)* _____ at 10:30 A.M. for Hawaii. We
             (3)

(spend) _____ the night there, and we *(fly)* _____ again
     (4)   (5)

the next morning. We *(arrive)* _____ in Hong Kong at 4 P.M. on
            (6)

Saturday. Anyway, that's why I *(not / go)* _____ to your party next
            (7)

Saturday. Sorry about that! I hope you'll have a good time.

Your friend,
Monica

Moving Up

4 Look at the pictures and read the questions. Then write the answers. Use contractions when possible.

1. Are Jack and Kenji going to play tennis?
   No, they aren't. They're going to play soccer.

2. Is Ramona going to listen to the radio?

   _____

3. Is Ruben going to buy some sandwiches?

   _____

4. Are Mr. and Mrs. Jones going to travel by plane?

   _____

5. Is Rosa going to wear jeans and a sweatshirt tonight?

   _____

Reaching for the Top

5 Read Kenji's schedule. Then read the answers. Write questions with *be going to* on the lines. Use contractions when possible.

Monday	
Morning	Go to the gym at 9:30 A.M.
Afternoon	Meet Clara at Tony's Café!
Evening	Finish school project.
Tuesday	
Morning	Call Daniel and invite him to the party.
Afternoon	Take bus at 2:30 P.M. to the dentist.
Evening	Have dinner with Clara at Mario's Pizza.

1. *What's he going to do on Monday morning?*

   Go to the gym.

2. _____

   At 9:30 A.M.

3. _____

   Clara.

4. _____

   Finish his school project.

5. _____

   Call Daniel and invite him to the party.

6. _____

   At 2:30 P.M. on Tuesday.

7. _____

   By bus.

8. _____

   Have dinner with Clara.

9. _____

   At Mario's Pizza.

Communication

Getting Started

6 Look at the pictures. Then complete the conversations. Use the words from the box.

too big	~~too small~~	too loose
too short	too tight	

1. A: What do you think of this jacket?

   B: Hmm. *I think it's too small.*

2. A: What do you think of these pants?

   B: I think _____.

3. A: Do you like this T-shirt?

   B: _____.

4. A: Do you like this dress?

   B: _____.

5. A: What do you think of this jacket?

   B: I think the sleeves _____.

Moving Up

7 Suppose that you won the trip in the advertisement below. Complete the conversation. Write sentences with *be going to*. Use contractions.

> **Win a five-day trip to Disney World in Orlando, Florida! June 3–7**
>
> ✷ Stay at the Disney Boardwalk Resort.
> ✷ Visit three exciting theme parks: Magic Kingdom®, Epcot®, and Disney's Animal Kingdom®!
> ✷ See 'NSync in concert.

You: I'm really excited. I'm going to Disney World!

Friend: You are? When are you going to leave?

You: (1) *I'm going to leave on June 3.*

Friend: Fantastic! Just for a couple of days?

You: (2) _____

Friend: Five days! Where are you going to stay?

You: (3) _____

Friend: What theme parks are you going to visit?

You: (4) _____

_____

Friend: Awesome! What else are you going to do?

You: (5) _____

_____

Reaching for the Top

8 Imagine that you and a friend are going to a party. In your notebook, write a conversation. Discuss what you are going to wear.

7 You were awesome, Alex!

Vocabulary

Getting Started

1 Look at the calendars below. Imagine that today is May 10.
Answer the questions. Write the dates on the lines.

✧ APRIL ✧						
S	M	T	W	Th	F	S
		1	2	3	4	5
6	7	8	9	10	11	12
13	14	15	16	17	18	19
20	21	22	23	24	25	26
27	28	29	30			

✪ MAY ✪						
S	M	T	W	Th	F	S
				1	2	3
4	5	6	7	8	9	(10)
11	12	13	14	15	16	17
18	19	20	21	22	23	24
25	26	27	28	29	38	31

1. Antonio's birthday was <u>one week ago</u>. What date was it? _____May 3_____

2. Alana's school visit to the museum was <u>two days ago</u>. What date was it? _____

3. Sara went to a concert <u>last Saturday night</u>. What date was it? _____

4. Matthew's math test was <u>yesterday</u>. What date was it? _____

5. Emmi started dance classes <u>three weeks ago</u>. What date was it? _____

Moving Up

2 Complete the sentences with past-time markers.

1. It's sunny right now, but _a few hours ago_ it rained.

2. It is the year 2003. The year 1998 was _____.

3. _____, we didn't go on vacation. This year, we are going to go to Florida.

4. They're tired this morning. They were out late _____.

5. _____, she was 14. This year, she is 15.

6. It's already March! His birthday was _____, in February.

7. Pablo wasn't in school _____. He was sick. He's here today and feels better.

Grammar

Getting Started

3 Complete the sentences with the simple past form of the verbs in the box. Use each verb only once.

finish	talk	hate	call	clean
watch	play	wash	listen	
~~visit~~	like	cook	help	

1. My cousin __*visited*__ us on Saturday. He and I _____ a few video games.

2. Last night Maria _____ her friend on the phone, and they _____ for a long time. Then she _____ to her new CDs and _____ the Olympics on TV. She especially _____ the ice-skating part.

3. First, Pedro _____ his homework. Next, he _____ his room. Then he _____ his mom with dinner. After dinner, he _____ the dishes.

4. The first time I tried beans, I _____ them, but now I like them. I _____ some last night.

4 Rewrite the sentences. Make the <u>underlined</u> simple past tense verbs negative. Use contractions when possible.

1. Clara <u>wanted</u> to buy the hat for her mother.
   Clara didn't want to buy the hat
   for her mother.

2. You <u>liked</u> that TV show last night.
   _____
   _____

3. Yesterday, we <u>played</u> soccer at the park.
   _____
   _____

4. I <u>cried</u> at the end of the movie.
   _____
   _____

5. Rachel's grandchildren <u>hugged</u> her at the party.
   _____
   _____

6. Mateo <u>studied</u> for three hours last night.
   _____
   _____

5 Read each question. Then circle the letter next to the correct answer.

1. Did the movie start at 7 P.M.?
   a. Yes, it started.
   b. Yes, it did.
   c. Yes, it starts.

2. Did you watch the baseball game after school yesterday?
   a. No, I didn't.
   b. No, I don't.
   c. No, I didn't watched it.

3. Did he miss the bus this morning?
   a. Yes, he missed.
   b. Yes, he have.
   c. Yes, he did.

4. Did you enjoy the rock concert?
   a. No, I didn't enjoy it.
   b. No, I don't enjoy it.
   c. No, I didn't enjoyed it.

5. Did they play soccer in the park last weekend?
   a. Yes, they have.
   b. Yes, they are playing.
   c. Yes, they did.

6. Did Kim walk to school this morning?
   a. No, she doesn't.
   b. No, she didn't.
   c. No, she isn't.

Reaching for the Top

6 Unscramble the questions. Then write them correctly on the lines.

1. I / borrow / did / jacket / black / When / your / ?

   When did I borrow your

   black jacket?

2. did / call / Who / Karen / ?

   _____

   _____

3. like / that / Jesse / Why / movie / did / ?

   _____

   _____

4. go / Kenesha / When / Paula / did / and / to / concert / the / ?

   _____

   _____

5. for / dinner / prepare / you / did / What / ?

   _____

   _____

6. park / we / did / car / last / night / Where / the / ?

   _____

   _____

7 Make up answers to the questions in Exercise 6. Write them on the lines.

1. *You borrowed my black jacket last night.*

   _____

2. _____

   _____

3. _____

   _____

4. _____

   _____

5. _____

   _____

6. _____

   _____

8 Read the poster. Then complete the conversation.

Boston–New York Charity Bike Ride!

Date: September 15–17

Distance: 275 miles

Number of days: 3

Number of riders: 3,500

Mark: (*you / go on*) $\underline{Did\ you\ go\ on}$ a charity
   (1)
   bike ride last fall?

Ana: Yes, _____.
   (2)

Mark: When (*it / start*) _____?
   (3)

Ana: On September 15.

Mark: (*you / have*) _____ fun?
   (4)

Ana: Yes, _____. But it
   (5)
   (*require*) _____ a lot of work!
   (6)

Mark: How long (*take*) _____?
   (7)

Ana: Three days!

Mark: Where (*stay*) _____ at night?
   (8)

Ana: We stayed at campsites.

Mark: How many riders
   (*participate*) _____?
   (9)

Ana: About 3,500!

Mark: How (*you / return*) _____?
   (10)

Ana: I took the train home!

Communication

Getting Started

9 Circle the letter next to the best response for each statement.

1. Let's go to the movies!
   a. That's a good idea.
   b. Not really.

2. You gave me the wrong change.
   a. Yes, it is.
   b. You're right. I'm sorry.

3. Noriko is very funny. She makes me laugh.
   a. I agree.
   b. I don't know.

4. I think the new video game is a lot of fun.
   a. Oh, I do.
   b. I don't agree.

5. These cookies are great, aren't they?
   a. Not really.
   b. No, I'm not.

10 Number the lines of the conversation in the correct order. Then write the conversation on the lines.

_1_ I liked that movie. It was great!

_____ Because it was boring, wasn't it?

_____ Exciting? I almost fell asleep!

_____ OK. That's a good idea.

_____ Why did you hate it?

_____ I don't agree. I hated it.

_____ Well, we have different tastes in movies. Why don't we watch a comedy next time?

_____ Not really. It was exciting.

Reaching for the Top

11 Imagine that you and a friend went to the movies last night. Write a conversation you both have with another friend about the movie. Use the conversation in Exercise 10 as a model.

8 Did you hear the news?

Vocabulary

Getting Started

1 Look at the pictures. Then unscramble the letters to write the adjectives that describe the people.

 1. p h a y p _____*happy*_____

 2. d a s _____

 3. g r a n y _____

 4. p t u s e _____

 5. u r i p d r e s s _____

 6. i c e d t e x _____

 7. s v o u n e r _____

 8. d r i t e _____

 9. d r e w r i o _____

Moving Up

2 Complete the sentences. Then write the correct words from Exercise 1.

1. She can't relax because she is afraid. She is ___*nervous*___.

2. Buying new clothes makes me feel very _____.

3. I got up at five o'clock. I'm very _____.

4. We're going to Brazil! I am really _____.

5. Another word for "unhappy" is _____.

6. You broke your brother's video game. He is very _____.

7. I was very _____ when my friends gave me a party!

8. Sue is _____ because she can't go to the school dance.

9. I'm not _____ about the test. I studied hard for it.

Grammar

Getting Started

3 Write the simple past form of the irregular verbs.

Base form	Simple past form		Base form	Simple past form
1. be	was/were		9. go	_____
2. buy	_____		10. have	_____
3. come	_____		11. hear	_____
4. do	_____		12. hold	_____
5. drive	_____		13. sleep	_____
6. feel	_____		14. stand	_____
7. give	_____		15. tell	_____
8. get	_____			

4 Complete the story. Use the simple past form of the verbs in the box. One verb is used three times.

get	drive	be	buy	stand
go	do	give	sleep	

Last week, I __went__ to a Destiny's
        (1)
Child concert with my friend, Lisa. Her Mom

_____ us to the concert. When we _____
   (2)   (3)
there, Lisa's mom _____ us some money,
                        (4)
and we _____ in line at the entrance. Lisa
            (5)
was very hungry, so she _____ a
                              (6)
hamburger.

The concert _____ fantastic! Destiny's
                (7)
Child sang all their hit songs and _____
                                        (8)
some great new dance routines.

   After the concert, we _____ very tired
                              (9)
but happy. In fact, I _____ so tired that I
                          (10)
_____ until 11 o'clock the next morning!
  (11)

5 Complete the sentences with *and*, *but*, or *so*.

1. Anna can swim, __but__ her brother can't.

2. I like bananas, _____ I always have two every day.

3. Their house is small, _____ it is also old.

4. I love skateboarding, _____ my friend doesn't like it.

5. I wasn't tired, _____ I didn't go to bed early.

6. My computer doesn't work, _____ I'm using my father's laptop.

7. My room is small, _____ it has two big windows.

8. Sue didn't have time, _____ she didn't go shopping.

9. Bill speaks Russian, _____ he speaks Japanese, too.

Moving Up

6 Make sentences. Choose a line from Column A, a word from Column B, and a line from Column C. Then write the sentences.

A	B	C
1. Last night I saw your sister,		a. she was ready for the test.
2. Lorna studied all day,	but	b. I missed the beginning of the movie.
3. Mario felt sick,		c. she didn't see me.
4. I ran all the way to the theatre,	so	d. he went home early from school.
5. They got in the car,		e. I didn't sleep well.
6. You thought the game was exciting,	and	f. I drove them to the concert.
7. I was worried about the English test,		g. I thought it was boring.

1. *Last night I saw your sister, but she didn't see me.* _____

2. _____

3. _____

4. _____

5. _____

6. _____

7. _____

Reaching for the Top

7 Complete the sentences. Write the simple past of the verb in the affirmative or negative form.

1. I didn't tell a lie; I (*tell*) _____*told*_____ the truth.

2. Mom was just tired; she (*be*) _____ sick.

3. Mark (*break*) _____ his leg; he didn't break his arm.

4. They (*buy*) _____ CDs; they didn't buy video games.

5. We didn't have hot dogs; we (*have*) _____ pizza.

6. The boys didn't go to the park; they (*go*) _____ to the gym.

7. You (*give*) _____ us cookies; you didn't give us cake.

8. Dad got up at eight o'clock; he (*get up*) _____ at six.

Communication

Getting Started

8 Number the lines of the conversation in the correct order.

Cora

____ Oh, really. Was he cute?

____ Well, I think you need more confidence.

__1__ Hey, Teri! How was your first driving lesson?

____ Where did you drive?

____ In the parking lot? That's not very exciting!

Teri

____ We drove around in the parking lot.

____ I know, but I didn't want to go on the roads.

____ Not really, but he's a good teacher.

__2__ It was OK. My instructor was nice.

____ I need a lot of confidence!

Moving Up

9 Write the conversations using the cues.

1. exam / ?

   A: _How was the exam?_

   difficult

   B: _It was difficult._

   you / pass / ?

   A: _Did you pass?_

   not / know / think /do / OK

   B: _I don't know. I think I did OK._

2. trip / ?

   A: _____

   boring

   B: _____

   you / drive / ?

   A: _____

   No / Dad / all the way

   B: _____

3. the meal / ?

   A: _____

   fantastic

   B: _____

   What / eat / ?

   A: _____

   a steak

   B: _____

Reaching for the Top

10 Write down a conversation you had with a friend about a movie, a meal, a trip, or something that happened in class. Use the conversations in Exercise 9 as models.

_____
_____
_____
_____
_____
_____
_____
_____
_____
_____
_____
_____
_____
_____
_____

Study Corner

Looking Up Verb Forms in the Dictionary

Look up *kept* in a dictionary. You will find that it is the simple past form of *keep*.

11 Write the base forms of the verbs below. Use a dictionary if you need help.

1. understood   _understand_

2. wrote   _____

3. paid   _____

4. hid   _____

5. wore   _____

6. fought   _____

Skills Development 2

Reading

A strange experience at Versailles

1 Read the paragraphs. Then put them in the correct order. Write the numbers.

_____ (a) In 1901, two Englishwomen, Miss Moberly and Miss Gray went to France on a vacation. On a hot day in August, they visited the Palace of Versailles.

_____ (b) The men gave them directions in French, and the Englishwomen walked on until they reached the back of the Little Palace. There they saw a woman wearing a white hat and an old-fashioned dress.

_____ (c) After their visit to Versailles, Miss Moberly and Miss Gray realized that they had gone back to the time of the French Revolution. Many people disbelieved their story. What about you?

_____ (d) Late in the afternoon, they decided to visit the Little Palace, which is near the main palace, but they didn't know the way.

_1_ (e) Versailles, a town near Paris, is well known for the beautiful palace that King Louis XIV built for his family in the 1600s.

_____ (f) The woman in the white hat and the old-fashioned dress looked at the two tourists and then walked away.

_____ (g) Luckily, they saw two men dressed in long coats, three-cornered hats, and tights. The two women thought the clothes were odd, but they asked the men for directions to the Little Palace anyway.

_____ (h) Later, Miss Moberly and Miss Gray realized that the woman was Queen Marie Antoinette, because her portrait was in the main palace.

2 In your notebook, write the paragraphs in the correct order.

Vocabulary

3 **Find words in the text that have the following definitions. Write them on the lines.**

1. of a style that was popular years ago (paragraph b) *old-fashioned*

2. thought that something was not true (paragraph c) _____

3. famous (paragraph e) _____

4. unusual (paragraph g) _____

5. a picture of a person (paragraph h) _____

Comprehension

4 **Below is part of an interview with Miss Moberly and Miss Gray at Versailles. First, read the incomplete interview. Then, write the missing answers and questions.**

1. Where is Versailles?
   It's near Paris.

2. *Who built the Palace of Versailles?*
   Louis XIV.

3. _____
   Louis XIV and his family lived at Versailles during the 1600s.

4. _____
   We went there in August of 1901.

5. What was the weather like?
   _____

6. You saw two men. Why did you speak to them?
   _____

7. What clothes were the men wearing?
   _____

8. _____
   A woman in an old-fashioned dress.

9. _____
   She walked away.

10. _____
    The woman was Marie Antoinette.

11. How do you know that she was Marie Antoinette?
    _____

12. Which period of history did you go back to?
    _____

Writing

5 **Think about a ghost story you know well. Write it down on the lines below. Include the following information:**

- where the events took place
- when they took place
- who was involved
- what exactly happened

_____
_____
_____
_____
_____
_____
_____
_____
_____
_____
_____
_____
_____
_____
_____
_____
_____

Why didn't you call us?

Vocabulary

Getting Started

1 Circle six weather words in the puzzle.

```
C R Y R Y I S
L S P A N Y N
O M U I Y R O
U W I N D Y W
D E A Y N O Y
Y F O G G Y A
```

Moving Up

2 Look at the pictures. Then write about the weather.

1. It's foggy.   2. _____

3. _____   4. _____

5. _____   6. _____

Reaching for the Top

3 Write questions and answers about the weather. Use the cues.

1. Moscow

What's the weather like in Moscow?

It's foggy and snowy.

2. Paris

_____
_____

3. Sydney

_____
_____

4. Rio de Janeiro

_____
_____

Grammar

Getting Started

4 Match the two parts of each sentence. Write the letters.

1. _f_ We were lying on the beach
2. ____ While I was driving to school,
3. ____ My cell phone rang
4. ____ My uncle was playing soccer
5. ____ When mom got home,
6. ____ I was sleeping on the train
7. ____ When I saw Karen at the party,
8. ____ While Amy was sunbathing,

a. when somebody took my watch.
b. a bird landed on her stomach.
c. I was cleaning my room.
d. while we were watching the movie.
e. she was talking to Jim.
f. when it started to rain.
g. when he broke his leg.
h. a cat ran across the road.

5 Write what Clara was or wasn't doing in the picture below. Use the cues. Use contractions when possible.

1. wear / a hat
   She was wearing a hat.

2. carry / an umbrella
   She wasn't carrying an umbrella.

3. carry / a bag
   _____

4. go / to the bank
   _____

5. talk / on a cell phone
   _____

6. go / to a party
   _____

7. wear / a dress
   _____

8. drink / a soda
   _____

Moving Up

6 Complete the story. Write the simple past or the past continuous form of the verbs in parentheses. Use contractions when possible.

Last night at ten o'clock, Mario (*walk*) ___was walking___ home through the park when he
                                              (1)

(*hear*) _____ a noise. He (*start*) _____ to walk faster. A few minutes later, he
          (2)   (3)

(*hear*) _____ the noise again. Somebody (*follow*) _____ him! Mario
          (4)   (5)

(*decide*) _____ to call the police. While he (*search*) _____ in his backpack, he
            (6)   (7)

(*remember*) _____ that he (*not/carry*) _____ his cell phone. Now he
              (8)   (9)

(*start*) _____ to run. While he (*run*) _____, he (*fall down*) _____ and
           (10)   (11)   (12)

(*hurt*) _____ his leg. He (*sit*) _____ in the middle of the road when he
          (13)   (14)

(*feel*) _____ a hand on his shoulder. It was Melissa. "I'm sorry," she (*say*) _____. "I
          (15)   (16)

(*try*) _____ to scare you." "Well, congratulations! You (*succeed*) _____!"
         (17)   (18)

Mario shouted.

Reaching for the Top

7 Answer the questions about the story in Exercise 6. Write your answers on the lines.

1. What was Mario doing at ten o'clock last night?

   He was walking home through the park.

2. What did he do when he heard the noise?

   _____

3. While Mario was searching his backpack, what did he remember?

   _____

4. When did he hurt his leg?

   _____

5. What was Melissa trying to do at the time?

   _____

8 Answer these questions about yourself. Write the answers on the lines.

1. What were you doing last night at ten o'clock?

   _____

   _____

2. What were you doing an hour ago?

   _____

   _____

3. What were you doing at five o'clock yesterday afternoon?

   _____

   _____

4. What were you thinking about when you got to school this morning?

   _____

   _____

5. What were you doing at seven o'clock this morning?

   _____

   _____

Communication

Moving Up

9 Imagine that you were waiting for the bus when you saw an accident. Complete the conversation. Use the picture to help you.

Police Officer: So, what were you doing when the accident happened?

You: (1) *I was waiting for the bus* .

Police Officer: Did you see the accident?

You: (2) _____ .

Police Officer: What happened?

You: (3) _____

   _____

   when a car came out of the side street and hit him.

Police Officer: (4) _____

   _____?

You: No, he didn't. He drove away while the man was lying on the road.

Police Officer: Was the man wearing a helmet?

You: (5) _____ .

Police Officer: (6) _____?

You: I called an ambulance and then I went to help the man.

Police Officer: Thank you for your help.

Reaching for the Top

10 Imagine that you were in an accident while playing a sport. In your notebook, write a paragraph describing what happened. Use both the simple past and the past continuous.

10 Is he better than I ?

Grammar

Getting Started

1 Write the comparative and the superlative form of the adjectives.

	Comparative	Superlative
1. clean	cleaner	the cleanest
2. difficult	more difficult	the most difficult
3. bad	_____	_____
4. hot	_____	_____
5. happy	_____	_____
6. exciting	_____	_____
7. young	_____	_____
8. far	_____	_____

2 Write the comparative or the superlative form of the adjectives in parentheses.

1. Vatican City is the (*small*) <u>smallest</u> country in the world.

2. Athens is (*old*) _____ than Rome.

3. Angel Falls, in Venezuela, are (*high*) _____ than Niagara Falls.

4. The cheetah is the (*fast*) _____ animal in the world.

5. The Concorde travels (*fast*) _____ than the speed of sound.

6. What is the (*high*) _____ mountain in the world?

7. The Amazon River is (*long*) _____ than the Mississippi.

8. Russia is the (*large*) _____ country in the world.

Moving Up

3 Look at the picture. Write the comparative or the superlative form of the <u>underlined</u> adjectives.

Domingo   Sara   Chico   Flora

Domingo is <u>tall</u>.

1. Sara is ____taller____ than Domingo.

2. Chico is _____ than Sara.

3. Flora is _____ of them all.

Domingo's T-shirt is <u>loose</u>.

4. Sara's T-shirt is _____ than Domingo's.

5. Chico's T-shirt is _____ than Sara's.

6. Flora's T-shirt is _____ of them all.

Domingo's surfboard is <u>big</u>.

7. Sara's surfboard is _____ than Domingo's.

8. Chico's surfboard is _____ than Sara's.

9. Flora's surfboard is _____ of them all.

4 Complete the sentences with the comparative form of the adjectives.

1. She isn't very tall. Her sister is _____*taller*_____.
2. My backpack isn't very heavy. Yours is _____.
3. This city isn't very beautiful. Athens is _____.
4. Mike's school isn't very far. Ours is _____.
5. Jill isn't very good at music. She is _____ at sports.
6. Noriko's house isn't very big. She needs a _____ one.
7. The French movie wasn't very interesting. The Russian movie was _____.
8. The weather is not too bad today. It was _____ yesterday.

5 Complete the conversation with the words from the box.

as fast as	as tall as	as important as
~~as good as~~	as hard as	as talented as

Roberta: Hey, Jonathan. What's up?

Jonathan: I'm very upset! Mr. Samuels didn't pick me for the basketball team.

Roberta: That's too bad. I think you're
(1) ___*as good as*___ anyone else in the school.

Jonathan: Thanks, Roberta. I practice
(2) _____ anyone else, too.

Roberta: Did Frank Griffin get on the team?

Jonathan: Yes, he did.

Roberta: That's not fair. He isn't
(3) _____ you are.

Jonathan: Maybe not. But I know why he got picked instead of me. I'm not (4) _____
he is. He's 6 feet 2 inches.

Roberta: OK, he's taller. But he isn't
(5) _____ you are. You're the fastest kid in school.

Jonathan: Well, I guess Mr. Samuels thinks speed isn't (6) _____ height.

Reaching for the Top

6 Write sentences comparing Rosa and Kenji. Use the comparative form of the adjective or
as . . . as in your sentences.

Rosa	Kenji
1. I'm not very strong.	I'm strong.
2. I'm 5 feet 4 inches tall.	I'm 5 feet 4 inches tall.
3. I'm not a good skater.	I'm a good skater.
4. I'm 16 years old.	I'm 16 years old.
5. I live close to school.	I don't live close to school.
6. I have a very big family.	I don't have a big family.

1. *Kenji is stronger than Rosa.* _____

2. *Rosa is as tall as Kenji.* _____

3. _____

4. _____

5. _____

6. _____

7 Write your opinions using the superlative form of the adjectives in the phrases below.

1. (*good vacation*) *I think my best vacation was at Disney World.* _____

_____

2. (*dangerous sport in the world*) _____

_____

3. (*funny actor*) _____

_____

4. (*strong person I know*) _____

_____

5. (*popular music group*) _____

_____

6. (*bad movie*) _____

_____

Communication

Getting Started

8 Complete the conversation. Use sentences from the box.

> Which do you like better—the black jacket or the white one?
> But I like the high heels better.
> I think you look cool!
> Which pair of shoes is more fashionable—the high heels or the low heels?
> ~~Try that one. It's smaller.~~

Becky: What do you think of this top?

Elena: I think it's too big. (1) *Try that one. It's smaller.*

Becky: (2) _____.

Elena: I like the white one.

Becky: (3) _____

Elena: I think the low heels are more fashionable.

Becky: (4) _____

So, what do you think of my new look?

Elena: (5) _____

Reaching for the Top

9 Write a conversation between you and a friend in a clothing store. Use Exercise 8 as a model.

_____

_____

_____

_____

_____

_____

_____

_____

Study Corner

Guessing the Meaning of New Words

When you see a word you don't know, ask questions about it.

• Is it similar to a word in my language?
• Do I recognize a part of the word?
• Do the other words in the sentence help me guess the meaning of the word?
• Is it a noun, a verb, an adjective, or an adverb?

10 Guess the meaning of the underlined words. Write the words and the meanings in your notebook.

1. I like that dress. It's <u>fabulous</u>.
2. <u>Heat up</u> your dinner in the <u>microwave</u>.
3. She loves to play with kids. She makes extra money by <u>baby-sitting</u>.

11 You should get some rest.

Vocabulary

Getting Started

1 Complete the names of the parts of the body. Write the missing letters. Then identify the parts of the body in the picture. Write the numbers in the boxes.

1. f _i_ _n_ g e _r_
2. m __ u __ h
3. h __ a __
4. w a __ s __
5. s __ o __ __ d __ r
6. e __ r
7. __ t o __ a __ h
8. a __ k __ e
9. __ l __ __ w
10. f __ o __
11. b __ c __
12. l __ g

Moving Up

2 Complete the sentences with the names of the illnesses from the box.

stomachache	fever	~~headache~~
sore throat	cough	toothache

1. Maria, why do you need an aspirin? Do you have a ___*headache*___?

2. Frank is going to the dentist because he has a _____.

3. Ellen ate too much ice cream, and now she has a _____.

4. When Jim swallows food, his throat hurts. He has a _____.

5. Danny's temperature is very high. He has a _____.

6. I had to leave the theater because I had a _____, and I was disturbing everyone.

Reaching for the Top

3 Read the clues. Then write the words for the different parts of the body in the puzzle.

Across

1. This part of the body connects your head to your shoulders.
3. You have five of these on each hand.
5. You need these to see.
6. When you eat, your food goes here.
8. It's between your foot and your leg.
10. There are five of these on each foot.
11. It's in the middle of your arm.
13. Your teeth are in here.
15. It's behind you!
16. This joins your hand to your arm.

Down

2. It's in the middle of your leg.
3. The plural of *foot*.
4. This joins your arm to the rest of your body.
7. It's at the top of your leg.
9. This is for smelling things.
10. This is the "fattest finger."
12. Sometimes, you wear a belt around this part of your body.
14. You use these to hear.

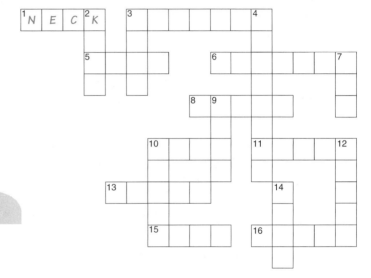

Grammar

Getting Started

4 Complete the students' opinions about homework. Write *should* or *shouldn't*.

2. Children need to play a lot. Children up to the age of 10 _____ have homework.

1. Children _____should_____ do homework in English and math every day.

4. Why _____ we do school work at home? There _____ be time for homework at school.

3. I think all children _____ do homework. You can learn a lot when you work at home.

5. I don't mind doing homework on weekdays, but we _____ have homework on weekends.

6. Why _____ I do homework in subjects I don't like? Teachers _____ give us homework in subjects that don't interest us.

7. We get two hours of homework every day. That's too much. We _____ get more than an hour.

Moving Up

5 Complete the conversations with *should* or *shouldn't* and a verb from the box.

feed give keep write ~~talk~~ put

1. A: Our math teacher gave us extra work because we talked during a test.

   B: You _shouldn't talk_ during a test!

2. A: I'm going to sit on the beach.

   B: You _____ some suntan lotion on.

3. A: They really love their dog!

   B: I know. But they _____ it expensive food all the time!

4. A: We found a fifty-dollar bill in the hallway. _____ we _____ it?

   B: No, you _____. You _____ it to a teacher.

5. A: My friend gave me a great birthday present.

   B: You _____ a thank-you note.

6 Read the sentences. Then write your advice using *should* or *shouldn't*.

1. A: I don't have time to do my homework in the evening.

   B: _You should do your homework in the afternoon._

2. A: I hurt my ankle while I was running down the stairs.

   B: _____

3. A: These shoes are too small.

   B: _____

4. A: She's really good at tennis, but she doesn't practice very often.

   B: _____

5. A: I don't like the new restaurant on High Street.

   B: _____

Reaching for the Top

7 Look at the two charts. Then write sentences telling what Maria used to do and what she just started to do.

Things Maria Used to Do	Things Maria Just Started to Do
drink soda	go to the gym
eat junk food	eat fresh fruit
go to bed late	jog
watch TV a lot	study a lot
take the bus to school	walk to school

1. (*soda*)

   She used to drink soda.

2. (*the gym*)

   She didn't use to go to the gym.

3. (*junk food*)

   _____

4. (*fresh fruit*)

   _____

5. (*bed*)

   _____

6. (*jog*)

   _____

7. (*TV*)

   _____

8. (*study*)

   _____

9. (*bus*)

   _____

10. (*walk*)

   _____

Communication

Getting Started

8 Complete the conversations with advice. Write sentences using *should* or *shouldn't* and an expression from the box.

wear helmets	study harder	~~call the dentist~~
stay up late	watch TV	wear shorts

1. A: I broke my tooth.
   B: *You should call the dentist.*

2. A: It's colder outside today.
   B: _____

3. A: We want to ride our bicycles.
   B: _____

4. A: Dan has to get up early tomorrow.
   B: _____

5. A: Rita wants to do better on her next math test.
   B: _____

6. A: They have a lot of homework.
   B: _____

Moving Up

9 Number the lines of the conversation in the correct order. Then write the conversation on the lines.

_____ I feel that I'm getting sick. What should I do?

__1__ Hi, Gary! You don't look good. Do you feel OK?

_____ Anything else?

_____ What's the matter?

_____ Yeah, you're right. I also have a bad headache.

_____ No, I don't.

_____ Maybe you should take some aspirin.

_____ Yes, if you don't get better in a couple of days, you should see your doctor.

_____ First, you should go home and get some rest.

_____
_____
_____
_____
_____
_____
_____
_____
_____
_____
_____
_____
_____

Reaching for the Top

10 In your notebook, write a conversation between you and a friend who needs advice. Choose one of the situations below, or use your own idea. Use the conversation in Exercise 9 as a model.

He or She . . .
• lost a friend's new CD.
• is very worried about the next English test.
• wants to ask a friend to go out.

12 Will you call us?

Grammar

Getting Started

1 Complete the sentences. Write the pronouns with *will*. Use contractions.

1. (*He*) _____He'll_____ be late for class.

2. (*She / not*) ___She won't___ clean her room.

3. (*It*) _____ be warmer tomorrow.

4. (*They*) _____ come to my party.

5. (*It / not*) _____ rain. Don't worry!

6. (*We*) _____ go to the dentist tomorrow.

7. (*He / not*) _____ come tomorrow.

8. I'm tired. (*I / not*) _____ stay up late.

2 Complete the sentences. Write *will* and a verb from the box. Use contractions when possible.

wake up	have	take	go
practice	leave	meet	get

1. Matt __will wake up__ at 6:30 A.M.

2. First, he _____'ll take_____ a shower.

3. Next, he _____ breakfast.

4. Then he _____ dressed.

5. At 7:30 A.M., he _____ for school.

6. He _____ his friend in front of his house.

7. They _____ to school by bus.

8. After school, they _____ soccer.

3 Unscramble the words to write questions. Then write short answers. Use the sentences in Exercise 2 to help you.

1. at / Matt / Will / 6 A.M. / wake up / ?
   Will Matt wake up at 6 A.M.?
   No, he won't.

2. a / shower / take / he / Will / ?
   _____
   _____

3. dressed / breakfast / Will / before / he / get / ?
   _____
   _____

4. meet / he / Will / friend / his / ?
   _____
   _____

5. to / by bus / they / go / Will /school / ?
   _____
   _____

6. football / after / Will / practice / they / school / ?
   _____
   _____

4 Complete the conversations. Circle the correct words.

1. A: Where's Juan?

   B: Don't worry. He (*might* / *will*) be here. He's never late.

2. A: Why isn't Sarah at school today?

   B: I don't know. She (*might* / *will*) be sick.

3. A: Do I need an umbrella?

   B: No, you don't. It (*might* / *won't*) rain.

4. A: What's the matter?

   B: My car (*may not* / *won't*) start.

5. A: What's wrong with Abdul?

   B: I'm not sure. He (*may* / *will*) be worried about his test.

6. A: So long, Roberto. Keep in touch.

   B: I (*might* / *will*) write to you every day. I promise.

7. A: How do you use this computer?

   B: It's easy. I (*will* / *might*) show you.

8. A: I need to talk to Magali, but I can't find her.

   B: Check in the library. She (*will* / *might*) be there with Paula.

5 Complete Sandra's e-mail to her friend Tania in Rio de Janeiro. Use *will*, *may*, or *might*.

Moving Up

6 Complete the conversations with *will* or *won't* and a verb, if needed. Use contractions when possible.

1. A: The movie starts at 7 P.M.

   B: That means we ___'ll have___ time to shop.

2. A: Look at those clouds!

   B: Don't worry. It _____.

3. A: I am tired. I don't want to go out tonight.

   B: Just rest a little and you _____ better.

4. A: The paintings were beautiful, but we didn't see all of them.

   B: Well, we _____ next week if you like.

5. A: Let's walk to the beach.

   B: Good idea. It's not very far, so it _____ long.

6. A: Anna, the phone is ringing.

   B: OK, I _____ it.

7. A: I think that Karen _____ a good grade on her test.

   B: No, she _____. She didn't study at all.

8. A: How _____ you _____ home from Maria's house?

   B: I _____ home. My house isn't very far.

Hi Tania,

How are you doing? Guess what? I have a big surprise for you. Next month, my parents and I
(1) _____*will*_____ go on vacation. To Rio! My father bought the tickets yesterday. We
(2) _____ arrive in Rio on July 10th and we (3) _____ stay there for a week. I'm
very happy because I (4) _____ finally have the chance to meet you. But there is more. I'm
not sure yet, but my friend Graciela and her family (5) _____ go too. Remember her
brother, Alex? He's really good looking, and you (6) _____ have the chance to meet him.
I'm sure you (7) _____ like him. We (8) _____ definitely have a great time
together. We don't have definite plans after Rio de Janeiro. We (9) _____ go to São Paulo or
to Belo Horizonte. I want to stay in Rio the whole time, but my parents want to see other cities in
Brazil. I hope they have a great time in Rio and decide to spend another week there.

Best,
Sandra

7 Complete the conversation. Write sentences with the pronoun *I*, the word *may* or *might*, and one of the phrases from the box.

go to Miami
not go to summer school at all
just stay home and watch TV
ask Nancy
just order a pizza
take a trip

Josh: Are you going to go to summer school?

Katie: No, I'm not. (1) *I might not go to summer school at all.*

Josh: What are you going to do instead?

Katie: I don't know. (2) _____

_____

Josh: To where?

Katie: I'm not sure yet. (3) _____

_____

Josh: Who are you going to go with?

Katie: I don't know. (4) _____

_____

Josh: Are you going out tonight?

Katie: Probably not. (5) _____

_____

Josh: What are you having for dinner then?

Katie: I don't know. (6) _____

_____

Reaching for the Top

8 Write true sentences about yourself. Use a word or expression from the box and the cues.

will	may	may not
won't	might	might not

1. be in bed by 9:30 P.M. tomorrow
   I won't be in bed by 9:30 P.M. tomorrow.

2. go on vacation next summer
   _____

3. be asleep at 2 A.M. tomorrow
   _____

4. have fish for dinner tonight
   _____

5. go to school tomorrow
   _____

6. go to the movies next weekend
   _____

Vocabulary

Getting Started

9 Find the summer activities. Match a verb in Column A with a phrase in Column B. Write the letters.

	A	B
_c_	1. learn	a. abroad
___	2. find	b. summer classes
___	3. take	c. a new skill
___	4. discover	d. summer camp
___	5. attend	e. in athletics
___	6. travel	f. a job
___	7. train	g. a hobby

Reaching for the Top

10 In your notebook, write seven true sentences about yourself. Tell what you *will/won't* and *might/might not* do this summer. Use phrases from Exercise 9 if possible.

Examples: <u>*I might find a job this summer.*</u>
<u>*I won't take summer classes.*</u>

Communication

Moving Up

11 Number the lines of the conversation in the correct order. Then write the conversation on the lines.

Tony

_____ Then come with me. It'll be fun!

_____ First, I'll just take it easy. Then I want to go abroad.

_____ Oh, yeah? What kind of job?

_____ I have cousins in Mexico, so I'll definitely go there.

__1__ Well, school is out. Do you have any plans for the summer?

Chuck

_____ I think I might work in a bookstore. What are *you* going to do?

_____ I'd love to go to Mexico.

_____ OK, sure. I'll get a job when we come back.

_____ Where will you go?

__2__ No, not really. But I might try to find a job.

Tony: <u>*Well, school is out. Do you have any*</u>
<u>*plans for the summer?*</u>

Chuck: <u>*No, not really. But I might try to find*</u>
<u>*a job.*</u>

Tony: _____

_____

Chuck: _____

_____

Tony: _____

_____

Chuck: _____

_____

Tony: _____

_____

Chuck: _____

_____

Tony: _____

_____

Chuck: _____

Reaching for the Top

12 In your notebook, write a conversation between you and a friend. Discuss your plans for next weekend, for a summer vacation, or for when you finish high school. Use the conversation in Exercise 11 as a model.

Study Corner

Main Stress in Words
When you write new words in your vocabulary notebook, it is useful to mark the main stress. Knowing the main stress will help you pronounce the word.

13 Write down a list of five occupations. Mark the main stress in each word. When you find a new word describing an occupation, add it to your list.
Examples: secretary, director.

Reading

From Ireland to America

The summer of 1845 was very cold and rainy in Ireland. The potato crop failed and people had nothing to eat. Almost a quarter of the population died of famine or disease.

A lot of people left Ireland to look for a better life in America. They crossed the Irish Sea to Liverpool, England, where they hoped to take a ship across the Atlantic.

In Liverpool, there were immigrants from all over Europe. They were all waiting to sail to America.

In 1845, Mary O'Casey and her family left Ireland, too. It took the family 36 hours to travel to Liverpool. This is Mary's story.

✢

At last we arrived in Liverpool! A man came up to us at the dock. "Do you need accommodations?" he asked. "I know a good place for you. It's cheap and it's not too far. You can walk there in about five minutes."

"Can you give us directions?" I asked.

"Just go down Main Street and turn left at the second corner. You can't miss it. By the way, do you have your tickets for America? I can get them for you at a special price."

We gave the man some money for the tickets. While we were walking to the hotel, he disappeared into a bakery. We thought he was getting the tickets.

We followed the man's directions, but we didn't find the hotel. In fact, we never saw the man or our money again. Later, we found out that he belonged to a gang called "The Forty Thieves."

We had just enough money for the tickets and some food, but not for accommodations. So we slept by the dock for five days, waiting for our ship.

There were 476 people on board our ship, the *Lucania*. While we were crossing the Atlantic, 158 died of fever. The trip took fourteen weeks.

When we arrived in New York, my husband and I found work on a farm. Our son is learning to read and write now. One day we might take him back to Ireland to show him where he used to live.

Vocabulary

1 Match each word in Column A with its definition in Column B. Write the letters.

A	B
_f_ 1. dock	a. a place to stay overnight
___ 2. population	b. people who steal money and things from others
___ 3. immigrants	c. was part of
___ 4. famine	d. not expensive
___ 5. accommodations	e. the number of people who live in a country
___ 6. belonged	f. the area next to the water that receives ships
___ 7. cheap	g. a time of great hunger
___ 8. thieves	h. people who come to another country to live

Comprehension

2 Read the sentences. Then put the events in the correct order. Write the numbers.

___ a. In Liverpool, they met a man who knew about some cheap accommodations.

___ b. The trip took fourteen weeks.

___ c. The man left them and did not return.

___ d. They travelled to Liverpool, England.

___ e. Finally, they took a ship to America.

___ f. While they were waiting for their ship, they slept on the dock.

___ g. They gave the man some money.

_1_ h. The O'Casey family left Ireland because of the potato famine.

___ i. They now had five days to wait for the next ship, but they didn't have a place to stay.

3 Complete the notes. Write the missing information about the O'Casey family.

1. Reasons for leaving Ireland: _the potato famine; to find a better life in America_

2. First part of trip: From _____ to _____

   Travel time: _____

   Number of days in Liverpool: _____

   Accommodations in Liverpool: _____

3. Second part of trip: From _____ to _____

   Travel time: _____

   Plans for the future: _____

Writing

4 In your notebook, write about immigrants in your country. Answer the following questions:

- Where are they from?
- Why did they leave their native country?
- When did they leave their native country?
- Why did they choose their new country?
- How did they travel to their new country?
- What problems did they have while they traveled?
- What problems did they have when they arrived?
- Do they seem happy now in their new country?

Grammar Builder

Grammar Highlights

Review of *be*

Affirmative statements

I	**am**	
You	**are**	} **strong.**
He, She, It	**is**	
We, They	**are**	

Negative statements

I	**am not**	
You	**are not**	} **strong.**
He, She, It	**is not**	
We, They	**are not**	

> **Remember:** The contractions of pronouns and *be* are: *I'm, you're, he's, she's, it's, we're,* and *they're.*

> **Remember:** The words *am* and *not* are not contracted (shortened) after the subject pronoun *I* : *I am not* or *I'm not,* not *I amn't*

Yes/No questions

Am	I	
Are	you	
Is	he, she, it	} **tall?**
Are	we, they	

Short affirmative/negative answers

Yes, you **are.** / No you**'re not.**

Yes, I **am.** / No, I**'m not.**

Yes, he **is.** / No, he**'s not.** (No, he **isn't.**)
Yes, it **is.** / No, it**'s not.** (No, it **isn't.**)

Yes, we **are.** / No, we**'re not.** (No, we **aren't.**)
Yes, they **are.** / No, they**'re not.** (No, they **aren't.**)

Information questions

Who is he?
What is your address?
When is the party?
Where is she?
How old are you?

Answers

He's my friend.
It's 2429 Pearl Street.
On Saturday night.
She's at the library.
I'm 14.

> **Remember:** *Who + is = Who's* (*Who's he?*)
> *What + is = What's* (*What's her name?*)
> *Where + is = Where's* (*Where's her house?*)

Possessive pronouns

Possessive adjectives

my	**My** hat is on the table.
your	**Your** CD is on the table.
his	**His** jacket is on the table.
her	**Her** hat is on the table.
our	**Our** keys are on the table.
their	**Their** books are on the table.

Possessive pronouns

mine	That hat is **mine.**
yours	That CD is **yours.**
his	That jacket is **his.**
hers	That hat is **hers.**
ours	Those keys are **ours.**
theirs	Those books are **theirs.**

> **Remember:** Possessive adjectives are always followed by a noun. Possessive pronouns are not followed by a noun; they stand alone. It's **my video game.** It's **mine.**

Practice

Review of *be*

Affirmative and negative statements

1 Complete Sofia's e-mail. Write the correct form of the verb *be*. Use contractions when possible.

Hi, Emily,

My name _____ Sofia. I _____ 14 years
      (1)   (2)
old. I _____ in the seventh grade at Wheeler
      (3)
High School in Queens, New York. I _____
                                       (4)
tall and thin. I have long, wavy brown hair and
blue eyes. I wear glasses. There are five people
in my family: my father, my mother, my brother,
my sister, and me. My father's name _____
                                      (5)
Juan. He _____ a salesman for a computer
         (6)
company. My mother's name _____ Rosa.
                            (7)
She _____ a teacher. My sister's name
    (8)
_____ Linda; she _____ 16 years old. My
 (9)   (10)
brother, Juan, _____ 19 years old. He
               (11)
_____ in college. My sister and brother
 (12)
_____ cool!
 (13)

My best friend at school _____ Barbara. We
                          (14)
love basketball. We _____ on the girls'
                     (15)
basketball team. We (*negative form*) _____
                                       (16)
the best players, but we have a lot of fun
playing.

You _____ my new key pal, so please e-mail
    (17)
me soon. Tell me about yourself and your
family.

   Sofia

2 Complete the sentences. Write the correct form of the verb *be*. Use contractions when possible.

1. I (*negative form*) <u>'m not</u> 15 years old. I
   _____ 12 years old.

2. They (*negative form*) _____ in my high
   school. They _____ in your high school.

3. You (*negative form*) _____ from Mexico. You
   _____ from Brazil.

4. He (*negative form*) _____ tall and thin. He
   _____ short and has a medium build.

5. Her hair (*negative form*) _____ brown. Her
   hair _____ blond.

6. We (*negative form*) _____ always serious.
   Sometimes we _____ funny.

7. I _____ in high school. I (*negative form*)
   _____ in college.

8. She _____ on the soccer team. She
   (*negative form*) _____ on the volleyball team.

Practice

Yes/No questions with short answers

3 Read Sofia's e-mail on page 65 again. Then write questions and short answers. Use the cues. If the answer is *No*, write the correct information. Use contractions when possible.

1. Sofia / 16 years old

   Is Sofia 16 years old?

   No, she's not. She's 14 years old.

2. Sofia / tall and thin

   _____

   _____

3. her father's name / Mike

   _____

   _____

4. her mother's name / Rosa

   _____

   _____

5. her father / a teacher

   _____

   _____

6. Sofia and Barbara / on a soccer team

   _____

   _____

7. Sofia and Barbara / best friends

   _____

   _____

8. Sofia / in ninth grade

   _____

   _____

Information questions with answers

4 Read the answers. Then write questions about the underlined words. Use *Who, What, When, Where,* or *How old.*

1. *Where are your mother and father?*

   My mother and father are on vacation in Caracas, Venezuela.

2. _____

   It's 10:30 P.M.

3. _____

   He's my brother.

4. _____

   My brother's name is Stuart.

5. _____

   It's April 14.

6. _____

   The concert is on Friday.

7. _____

   My brother is only 5 years old.

8. _____

   Our basketball practice is in the gym today.

9. _____

   My aunt is 22.

Practice

5 **Answer the questions about Sofia's e-mail on page 65. Write complete sentences. Use contractions when possible.**

1. How old is Sofia?

   She's 14 years old.

2. What grade is she in?

   _____

3. What is the name of her high school?

   _____

4. Where is her school?

   _____

5. What color is her hair?

   _____

6. Who is her best friend?

   _____

7. What sports team are Sofia and her friend on?

   _____

8. Who is her new key pal?

   _____

Possessive pronouns

6 **Complete the sentences with possessive pronouns.**

1. This is my new CD.

   This new CD is ___*mine*___.

2. That is his soccer ball.

   That soccer ball is _____.

3. That is your video game.

   That video game is _____.

4. Those are our backpacks.

   Those backpacks are _____.

5. Those are her comic books.

   Those comic books are _____.

6. Those are their cellular phones.

   Those cellular phones are _____.

7. This is my magazine.

   This magazine is _____.

7 **Complete the conversations. Circle the correct words.**

1. A: This cellular phone is cool. Is it (*your* / *yours*) or Clara's?

   B: It's (*my* / *mine*). (*Her* / *Hers*) is in her backpack.

2. A: Is this (*our* / *ours*) CD player, or is it (*their* / *theirs*)?

   B: It's (*our* / *ours*).

3. A: Can I use this cassette player?

   B: Ask Elena and Pablo. It's (*their* / *theirs*) cassette player.

Grammar Highlights

Count and noncount nouns

Count nouns can be counted.

Singular	Plural
an olive	olive**s**
a potato	potato**es**

Noncount nouns *cannot* be counted.
milk
butter
water
cheese
rice

> **Remember:** Use *an* before a singular count noun that begins with a vowel. Use *a* before a singular count noun that begins with a consonant.

> **Remember:** Do not use *a* or *an* before a plural count noun or a noncount noun.

> **Remember:** A noncount noun does not have a plural form.

There is/There are with *some* and *any*

Affirmative statements

There is a cookie
There's **some** milk   } on the table.
There are **some** cookies

Negative statements

There isn't a cookie
There isn't **any** milk   } on the table.
There aren't **any** cookies

Yes/No questions

Is there a cookie
Is there **any/some** milk   } on the table?
Are there **any/some** cookies

Short answers

Affirmative	Negative
Yes, there is.	No, there isn't.
Yes, there is.	No, there isn't.
Yes, there are.	No, there aren't.

> **Remember:** *There + is = There's*

> **Remember:** In questions, use *Is there any/some* with noncount nouns. Use *Are there any/some* with plural count nouns.

> **Remember:** Use *There is some* with a noncount noun. Use *There are some* with a plural count noun.

> **Remember:** Use *There isn't any* with a noncount noun. Use *There aren't any* with a plural count noun.

Practice

Count and noncount nouns

1 Write *C* next to the count nouns, and *NC* next to the noncount nouns.

<u>NC</u> 1. ice cream   _____ 7. tomato sauce   _____ 13. salt

<u>C</u>   2. chocolate chips   _____ 8. food   _____ 14. onion

_____ 3. nuts   _____ 9. cheese   _____ 15. cookie

_____ 4. juice   _____ 10. tomato   _____ 16. flour

_____ 5. apple   _____ 11. egg

_____ 6. potato   _____ 12. sugar

2 Read the sentences. Write *a* or *an* where necessary.

1. There is __*a*__ pizza in the oven.
2. There are _____ eggs in the refrigerator.
3. There is _____ orange juice in the glass.
4. There is _____ onion in the basket.
5. There are _____ toys on the floor.
6. There is _____ cookie on my plate.
7. There are _____ chocolate chips on this pizza!
8. There is _____ apple in the bowl.
9. There are _____ CDs in my bag.
10. There is _____ dog under the table.
11. There is _____ oil in the frying pan.
12. There is _____ car in front of the house.

There is/There are with *some* and *any*

Affirmative and negative statements

3 Look at the picture. Then complete the sentences. Write *There is, There are, There isn't,* or *There aren't.*

1. __*There is*__ a banana in the refrigerator.
2. _____ any eggs in the refrigerator.
3. _____ any sugar on the table.
4. _____ some milk in the refrigerator.
5. _____ some apples in the bowl.
6. _____ any cookies on the plate.

4 Look at the picture. Then write sentences using the cues. Use contractions when possible.

1. tomato (✓)   onion (✗)

   There's a tomato, but there isn't

   an onion.

2. eggs (✓)   apples (✗)

   _____

   _____

3. milk (✓)   juice (✗)

   _____

   _____

4. bananas (✓) pineapple (✗)

   _____

   _____

5. butter (✓)   olives (✗)

   _____

   _____

6. orange (✓)   lemonade (✗)

   _____

   _____

7. cheese (✓)   oil (✗)

   _____

   _____

Yes/No questions and short answers

5 Complete the questions with *Is there* or *Are there*.

1. *Is there* _____ an egg to bake a cake?
2. _____ salt for my french fries?
3. _____ olives on this pizza?
4. _____ a banana for Felix?
5. _____ toys for the kids?
6. _____ any water in this cup?
7. _____ potatoes in the box?
8. _____ any garlic in this omelette?
9. _____ any nuts in these cookies?
10. _____ an orange in this bag?

6 Write questions with *Is there* or *Are there* and the words in the box. Use *any* or *some* with noncount nouns and with plural count nouns. Use *a* or *an* with singular count nouns.

cookies	orange juice	cheese	eggs
orange	pineapple	banana	milk

1. *Are there any cookies?*
2. *Is there an orange?*
3. _____
4. _____
5. _____
6. _____
7. _____
8. _____

7 **Look at the picture below. Then write *Yes/No* questions and short answers using the cues.**

1. tomato

   Is there a tomato?

   Yes, there is.

2. onions

   Are there any onions?

   No, there aren't.

3. pineapples

   _____

   _____

4. apples

   _____

   _____

5. sugar

   _____

   _____

6. juice

   _____

   _____

7. cookies

   _____

   _____

8. banana

   _____

   _____

9. salt

   _____

   _____

10. nuts

    _____

    _____

11. orange

    _____

    _____

12. water

    _____

    _____

13. rice

    _____

    _____

14. oil

    _____

    _____

Grammar Highlights

Questions with *How much* and *How many*

Questions	Answers
Use *how many* with count nouns. **How many eggs** do you eat in a week?	Five. OR I eat five eggs in a week.
Use *how much* with noncount nouns. **How much butter** do I need for this recipe?	One cup. OR You need one cup of butter for that recipe.

Remember: Use *How much + be* to ask about the price of something. *How much* is an egg sandwich?

Expressions of measure

a loaf of (bread)
a carton of (juice)
a box of (cereal)
a bag of (rice)
a jar of (sauce)

a bottle of (water)
a pound of (chicken)
a gallon of (milk)
a bunch of (grapes)
a box of (strawberries)

Remember: Use expressions of measure in your answers to questions with *How much* and *How many*.
A: *How much* chicken do you want?
B: I want *a pound of* chicken, please.

Expressions of quantity with count and noncount nouns

Count nouns	Noncount nouns
a few strawberries	**a little** juice
a lot of cherries	**a lot** of milk
some grapes	**some** water

Remember: Use *a few* with count nouns and *a little* with noncount nouns. Use *a lot of* and *some* with both count and noncount nouns.

Practice

Questions with *How much* and *How many*

1 Complete the questions. Write *How much* or *How many*.

1. *How many* _____ classes does Kenesha have?
2. _____ eggs are in this recipe?
3. _____ soda do you drink in a day?
4. _____ cheese do you need for this recipe?
5. _____ slices of cheese does Vernon want in his sandwich?
6. _____ video games can you play today?
7. _____ lemonade did Kam Shing drink?
8. _____ homework do you have today?
9. _____ posters did Lu buy at the store?
10. _____ bottles of water are there in the package?

2 Unscramble the questions. Then write them correctly on the lines.

1. Maria / How many / guitars / does / have / ?
   How many guitars does Maria have?
2. How much / Raul / buy / did / yogurt / ?
   _____
3. want / you / How much / rice / do / ?
   _____
4. are / buying / How many / you / magazines / ?
   _____
5. want / for / How many / breakfast / eggs / you / do / ?
   _____

3 Read the answers. Then write the questions.

1. A: *How many new friends does Elena have?*
   B: Elena has three new friends.
2. A: _____
   B: Mateo eats three cups of yogurt a day.
3. A: _____
   B: There are 30 students in my English class this year.
4. A: _____
   B: I drink two small cartons of juice a day.
5. A: _____
   B: We need half a gallon of ice cream.
6. A: _____
   B: I spent a lot of money on these video games.

Expressions of measure

4 Complete the sentences with the expressions of measure from the box. Use each word only once.

bag	cans	glasses	piece
bowl	~~cup~~	head	pound
bunch	gallon	loaf	

1. Would you like a __cup__ of coffee?
2. Peter had a _____ of fruit and a _____ of cereal for breakfast.
3. We need a _____ of cheese for this recipe.
4. Mom used a _____ of chocolate chips to make cookies.
5. Do you drink eight _____ of water a day?
6. To make a salad, you need a _____ of lettuce.
7. My friend drinks three _____ of soda a day.
8. I have to buy a _____ of bread for dinner.
9. Anna wants a _____ of grapes for the fruit salad.
10. One _____ of milk a day is not enough for my family!

Expressions of quantity with count and noncount nouns

5 Read the questions. Then write *a little* or *a few* in the blank.

1. How much money does he have?
   a little

2. How many video games does she own?
   _____

3. How much tea do they want?
   _____

4. How many students does she know?
   _____

5. How much oil is in the bottle?
   _____

6. How much English do they speak?
   _____

7. How many mistakes did he make?
   _____

8. How many cookies did she eat?
   _____

9. How much do they like hip-hop music?
   _____

10. How much soda did he drink?
    _____

11. How many CDs did she buy?
    _____

12. How many olives are in the salad?
    _____

6 Read the answers. Then write questions using *How much* or *How many*.

1. _How many CDs do you have?_
   I only have a few CDs.

2. _____
   There is only a little water in the refrigerator.

3. _____
   I need a few bananas for the fruit salad.

4. _____
   Michael has a few friends in Mexico.

5. _____
   I have a little money in the bank.

6. _____
   The teacher has 25 students.

7 Complete each sentence. Circle the correct expression of quantity.

1. Emilio watched (*a little* / (*a few*)) news programs last night.
2. Louisa did (*a little* / *a few*) work today.
3. Did Elizabeth have (*a lot of* / *a few*) homework?
4. Did Brent buy (*a lot of* / *a little*) books at the bookstore?
5. Rita played (*a little* / *a few*) games with her grandchildren.
6. This recipe uses only (*a few* / *a little*) butter.
7. Alana watched (*a little* / *some*) TV shows with her mother.
8. Cara took (*a little* / *a lot of*) pens to school with her.
9. May I have (*a few* / *some*) pepper on my omelette?
10. I only have (*a little* / *a few*) time to play with you.
11. He started to work (*a little* / *a few*) weeks ago.
12. I'm thirsty. Can I have (*a few* / *some*) lemonade?
13. Would you like (*a little* / *a few*) ice cream?
14. David bought (*some* / *a little*) new shirts.

8 Write six sentences or questions. In each, use an expression of quantity and a count noun or a noncount noun from the box.

Examples: Do you eat *a lot of snacks* every day?

I want *some tomatoes* in my sandwich, please.

1. _____
2. _____
3. _____
4. _____
5. _____
6. _____

Expressions of quantity	Count nouns	Noncount nouns
a little	tomatoes	sugar
a few	snacks	milk
a lot of	classes	salad
some	nuts	cereal
	potatoes	water
	books	

Grammar Highlights

Gerunds as objects of verbs

Gerunds can be the objects of verbs.

I like **playing** soccer.
You love **swimming**.
Domingo hates **skateboarding**.
They enjoy **biking**.
She hates **writing** letters.
I enjoy **getting** e-mails from friends.

Remember: These verbs can be followed by gerunds:
enjoy   finish   go
hate   like   love

Remember: To form the gerund, add *-ing* to the base form of the verb.
read + *ing* = reading
Some verbs have spelling changes.
write + *ing* = writing
take + *ing* = taking
sit + *t* + *ing* = sitting
get + *t* + *ing* = getting

How often . . . ? and answers with frequency expressions

How often . . . ?	Answers with frequency expressions
How often does he/she play volleyball?	He/She plays volleyball { every day. / once a week. / twice a week. / three times a week.
How often do I/you/we/they exercise?	I/You/We/They never exercise.

Remember: *How often* asks about frequency—the number of times something happens or the number of times you do something.
In Seattle, it rains **every day**.
I swim **three times a week**.

Practice

Gerunds as objects of verbs

1   Complete the sentences with the gerund form of the verbs in parentheses.

1. Teresa loves *(ski)* _____skiing_____ down steep mountains.

2. My brother and I like *(play)* _____ soccer in the park.

3. You go *(swim)* _____ in your pool every morning. That's great!

4. Mateo and Amber enjoy *(ride)*_____ their new bikes.

5. Cody goes *(skateboard)* _____ every day.

6. Nori loves *(ice-skate)* _____ at the new ice rink.

7. Rosa and Mario always go *(in-line skate)* _____ after school.

8. Frank and I didn't like *(climb)* _____ the wall at the amusement park.

9. Hiroshi enjoys *(practice)* _____ gymnastics with his teammates.

10. I don't like *(play)* _____ volleyball. I never hit the ball over the net!

11. Did Maria finish *(clean)* _____ her room?

12. Did they go *(snorkel)* _____ last weekend?

2   Complete the sentences. Write the gerund form of a verb of your choice. Use a different verb in each sentence.

1. I love _____shopping_____ for new clothes.

2. Do Madison and Amanda mind _____ their skates to the ice rink?

3. You like _____ the piano.

4. Sofia enjoys _____ in the chorus at school.

5. Does Mavis enjoy _____ to the movies on Friday nights?

6. He loves _____ dinner for his family! He's a great cook.

7. Did they finish _____ pair work in English class?

8. Antonio didn't finish _____ Unit 1 for his English class.

9. I enjoyed _____ that book about presidents of the United States.

10. Kyle and I love _____ basketball games on TV.

3 Complete the sentences with the gerund form of the verbs in the box.

travel	~~cook~~	ski
watch	play	do

1. Percy really likes _____cooking_____ breakfast for himself every morning.

2. Does Rosa like _____ down the tallest mountain?

3. Paula and I don't like _____ news programs on TV.

4. My mother and father love _____ to Mexico.

5. I hate _____ homework after dinner.

6. My friends and I enjoy _____ in the snow.

4 Complete the sentences. Write the gerund form of a verb of your choice. Use a different verb in each sentence.

1. Dan loves _____playing_____ in a rock-and-roll band.

2. The Molinas enjoy _____ in the winter.

3. I like _____ e-mails to my friends.

4. You don't like _____ in the ocean.

5. Anna and I stopped _____ in the library after school.

6. Did we finish _____ our homework?

5 Read the questions. Then write your answers using a gerund in each sentence.

1. Do you go skating sometimes after school?

_____

_____

2. What do you and your friends hate doing on weekends?

_____

_____

3. What do your classmates enjoy doing in their English class?

_____

_____

4. What does your family enjoy doing in the evening?

_____

_____

6 Write two sentences about something that you *like* doing and two sentences about something that you *don't like* doing. Use the verbs in parentheses and a gerund in each sentence.

Example: (*hate*) _I hate getting up early._

1. (*enjoy*) _____

2. (*like*) _____

3. (*don't like*) _____

4. (*hate*) _____

How often . . . ? and answers with frequency expressions

7 Write questions with *How often* and the cues.

1. they / visit their relatives in Barcelona / ?
   How often do they visit their relatives in
   Barcelona?

2. I / need to see the dentist / ?
   _____
   _____

3. Emilio / have English classes / ?
   _____
   _____

4. we / want to sing in the chorus / ?
   _____
   _____

5. you / practice gymnastics after school / ?
   _____
   _____

6. Grace / visit her grandmother in New York City / ?
   _____
   _____

8 Write statements about yourself. Use the cues and a frequency expression in each sentence.

1. go to work
   I go to work twice a week after school.

2. go shopping
   _____

3. drink orange juice
   _____

4. call my friends
   _____

5. watch soccer on TV
   _____

6. play video games
   _____

7. read the newspaper
   _____

8. go to the beach
   _____

9. work out at the gym
   _____

9 Write five questions with *How often.* Write the questions for a family member or a friend to answer.

Example: *How often do you go swimming?*

1. _____
2. _____
3. _____
4. _____
5. _____

Unit 5

Grammar Highlights

The present continuous

Information questions				Answers
Wh-word	**be**	subject	**verb + -ing**	
What	**are**	you	**reading**?	*Teen People.* [**I'm reading** *Teen People.*]
Where	**is**	he	**going**?	To the supermarket. [He**'s going** to the supermarket.]
Why	**are**	they	**leaving**?	They're tired. [They**'re leaving** because they're tired.]
Who (subject)	**be**		**verb + -ing**	
Who	**is**		**laughing**?	My brother. [My brother **is laughing**.]

Remember: Use the following rules to spell verbs in the present continuous tense.
1. For one-syllable words with a consonant, vowel, and consonant (CVC), double the last consonant and add -ing.
skip + p + ing = skipping
Do not double the last consonant if it is *w, x,* or *y.*
fix + ing = fixing
2. If a verb ends in a silent *e,* drop the *e* and add -ing.
take + ing = taking

The simple present and the present continuous

Simple present

I **walk** two miles every day.
She **takes** piano lessons twice a week.

Present continuous

I **am walking** to the store.
She **is playing** the piano now.

Information questions

What do you **do** on Friday nights?
What **are** you **doing** now?
What **do** they do at the park?
What **are** they **doing** at the park now?

Answers

I **go** to the movies.
I**'m reading** a book.
They **play** soccer.
They**'re riding** their bikes.

Remember: Use the present tense to talk about daily habits or usual activities.

Remember: Use the present continuous tense to talk about things that are happening now.

Practice

The present continuous

Information questions and answers

1 Look at the picture. What are the people doing? Write the present continuous form of the verbs.

1. My friends and I (*enjoy*) <u>are enjoying</u> ourselves in the park.

2. I (*sit*) _____ on the bench.

3. I (*write*) _____ a letter to my best friend, Antonio.

4. My dog, Skip, (*sleep*) _____ under the bench.

5. Isabel and Rico (*ride*) _____ their bikes along the path.

6. Lauren (*skate*) _____ right behind them.

2 First, look at the pictures. Then read the answers and write questions about the underlined words. Use *Who, What,* or *Where*.

1. <u>What are Tran and Jose doing?</u>

   They're playing basketball.

2. _____

   Carol is skating.

3. _____

   He's sitting under a tree.

4. _____

   He's reading a book.

5. _____

   They're playing Frisbee.

6. _____

   She's jogging.

7. _____

   He's talking on the telephone.

3 Read the answers. Then write questions about the underlined words. Use *Who, What, Where,* or *Why.*

1. *What is she making*

   for lunch?

   She's making a cheese sandwich for lunch.

2. _____

   _____

   We're going to the movies tonight.

3. _____

   _____

   They are riding their bikes in the park.

4. _____

   _____

   I'm painting a picture now.

5. _____

   _____

   Leon and Nicholas are playing basketball in the park now.

6. _____

   _____

   He's swimming in the pool at the gym.

7. _____

   _____

   They're practicing in the auditorium.

8. _____

   _____

   I'm laughing because you're funny.

The Simple Present and the Present Continuous

4 Complete the sentences. Write the simple present or the present continuous form of the verbs. Use contractions when possible.

1. How often do they (*go*) ___*go*___ to the beach?

2. My mom (*swim*) _____ for half an hour every morning.

3. Pablo (*play*) _____ soccer right now.

4. I (*study*) _____. Please be quiet.

5. Tina and I (*go*) _____ to camp together every summer.

6. What time do you (*study*) _____ piano after school?

7. Excuse me, we (*look for*) _____ Room 507.

8. We can't play outside. It (*rain*) _____.

9. Josh (*like*) _____ computer games.

5 Write the answers to the questions using the cues in parentheses. Use contractions when possible.

1. What is Pablo doing? (*clean / his room*)
   He's cleaning his room.

2. Where is everybody? (*they / play basketball*)

   _____

3. What's that noise? (*Tom / play his guitar*)

   _____

4. Why are you happy?
   (*be / in Anita's English class*)

   _____

5. How often do you go to the beach?
   (*go / once a week*)

   _____

6 Write the simple present or the present continuous form of the verbs. Use contractions when possible.

August 20, ____

Dear Aunt Clara,

Hi. How are you?

Mom, Dad, Felix, my friend Rebecca, and I (enjoy) _are enjoying_ (1) the day at Clearwater Beach. During the summer, we usually (come) _____ (2) to this beach on Saturdays.

Right now, Mom and Dad (sit) _____ (3) under an umbrella. They (read) _____ (4) their magazines. They usually (read) _____ (5) every day, even on Saturdays and Sundays. Felix (love) _____ (6) the ocean, so he (ride) _____ (7) the waves now. I can see him from my beach chair. I (write) _____ (8) this letter, and my friend Rebecca (wait) _____ (9) for me. She wants to jog along the beach. She and I always (do) _____ (10) lots of fun things together.

Please write me soon.

Love,

Julia

7 Write a letter or an e-mail to a friend or family member. Tell what you and your family are doing now. Also tell what you usually do. Use the letter in Exercise 6 as a model.

_____
_____
_____
_____
_____
_____
_____
_____
_____
_____
_____
_____

Unit 6

Grammar Highlights

Simple future: *be going to*

Affirmative statements

I **am going to**
You **are going to**
He **is going to**
She **is going to** } fall.
It **is going to**
We **are going to**
They **are going to**

Negative statements

I **am not going to**
You **are not going to**
He **is not going to**
She **is not going to** } fall.
It **is not going to**
We **are not going to**
They **are not going to**

Yes/No questions

Am I going to fall?
Are you going to fall?
Is he going to fall?
Is she going to fall?
Is it going to fall?
Are we going to fall?
Are they going to fall?

Affirmative answers

Yes, you are.
Yes, I am.
Yes, he is.
Yes, she is.
Yes, it is.
Yes, we are.
Yes, they are.

Negative answers

No, you **aren't**. (No, you **'re not**.)
No, **I'm** not.
No, he **isn't**. (No, he**'s not**.)
No, she **isn't**. (No, she**'s not**.)
No, it **isn't**. (No, it**'s not**.)
No, we **aren't**. (No, we **'re not**.)
No, they **aren't**. (No, they**'re not**.)

Information questions

Who **is going to go** to the concert?
What **are** you **going to wear** to the concert?
When **are** you **going to buy** your tickets?
Where **are** you **going to park** the car?
Why **are** you **going to take** the bus?
How **are** you **going to get to** the concert?

Practice

Simple future: *be going to*

Affirmative and negative statements

1 Write sentences with *be going to*. Use the cues and the verbs in the box. Use contractions when possible.

buy see go ~~send~~ leave rain wear

1. You / me a postcard from Barcelona
   You're going to send me a postcard
   from Barcelona.

2. Emilio and I / for Mexico City on September 4
   _____
   _____

3. I / to the shoe store this afternoon
   _____
   _____

4. My parents / me a bracelet for my birthday
   _____
   _____

5. Ana / Britney Spears in concert
   _____
   _____

6. It / on Monday
   _____
   _____

7. Yori / his new jeans tonight
   _____
   _____

2 Write sentences with *be going to* and the cues. Use contractions.

1. They / (*not*) take their coats. It / too warm
   They're not going to take their coats.
   It's too warm.

2. She / (*not*) wear her pink dress. It / too tight
   _____
   _____

3. You / (*not*) wear your red-and-white sweater. It / too small
   _____
   _____

4. He / (*not*) buy that hat. It / too big
   _____
   _____

5. I / (*not*) walk to the party. It / too cold
   _____
   _____

6. We / (*not*) shop at Fancy Clothes. It / too expensive
   _____
   _____

7. She / (*not*) buy that skirt. It / too long
   _____
   _____

Yes/No questions and answers

3 Complete the conversations. Write questions with *be going to* and the verbs in parentheses. Then complete the short answers.

1. A: <u>Are</u> you (*study*) <u>going to study</u> after school today?

   B: Yes, <u>I am</u>.

2. A: _____ Van and Kevin (*be*) _____ at the party tonight?

   B: Yes, _____.

3. A: _____ Ana (*swim*) _____ at the gym today?

   B: No, _____.

4. A: _____ Carlos (*buy*) _____ a present for his sister tomorrow?

   B: Yes, _____.

5. A: _____ we (*go*) _____ to the movies on Sunday?

   B: No, _____.

6. A: _____ I (*sing*) _____ in the concert on Friday night?

   B: No, _____.

Information questions

4 Read the answers. Then write questions about the underlined words with *be going to*. Use *Who, What, When, Where, Why,* and *How.*

1. <u>When are they going to go to the beach?</u>

   They're going to go to the beach <u>this afternoon</u>.

2. _____

   <u>Kathleen</u> is going to go to the mall.

3. _____

   I'm going to go <u>downtown</u> this evening.

4. _____

   Ana and I are going to <u>play soccer</u> on Sunday.

5. _____

   Marcia is going to get to the concert <u>by car</u>.

6. _____

   He's going to study in the library <u>because it's quiet there</u>.

5 Look at Magali's schedule for next week. Ask questions about her activities using *be going to* and *Who, What, Where, When,* and *How.*

MONDAY	TUESDAY	WEDNESDAY	THURSDAY	FRIDAY
Call Lidia on her birthday	Dentist appointment	Basketball practice at the gym	Piano practice at six	Buy concert tickets over the Internet

1. *Who is Magali going to call on Monday?* _____
2. _____
3. _____
4. _____
5. _____

6 You and your friends are planning to go to a party. Write information questions with *be going to* and the question words below. Then answer your questions.

1. Who *is going to go to the party?* _____

   Kevin and Mary are going to go

   to the party. _____

2. What _____

   _____

   _____

3. When _____

   _____

   _____

4. Where _____

   _____

   _____

5. Why _____

   _____

   _____

6. How _____

   _____

   _____

7 Read the sentences. Then write questions with *be going to* using the cues.

1. I'm very hungry. (*What / you / eat?*)

   What are you going to eat?

2. The sky is very dark. (*it / rain?*)

   Is it going to rain?

3. Bob's old car broke down. (*When / he / buy / a new car?*)

   _____

4. My birthday is tomorrow. (*you / have a party?*)

   _____

5. We're going to the movies. (*What / you / see?*)

   _____

6. Sue will be a university student next year. (*What / she / study?*)

   _____

7. It's very cold outside. (*it / snow?*)

   _____

8. Sue and Matt got new jobs. (*Where / they / work?*)

   _____

Unit 7

Grammar Highlights

The simple past tense: regular verbs

Affirmative statements

I **baked** a cake.
He/She **played** with me.
It **popped** open.
They **cried** at the end of
the movie.

Negative statements

I **did not bake** a cake.
He/She **did not play** with me.
It **did not pop** open.
They **did not cry** at the end of
the movie.

> **Remember:** *did + not = didn't*

> **Remember:** To form the simple past tense of most regular verbs, add -d or -ed.
> *bake + d = baked*
> *play + ed = played*

> **Remember:** To form the simple past tense of some regular verbs that end in a vowel + consonant, double the consonant and add -ed.
> *pop + p + ed = popped*
> *hop + p + ed = hopped*

> **Remember:** To form the simple past tense of verbs that end in a consonant + y, change the y to i and add -ed.
> *cry + i + ed = cried*
> *try + i + ed = tried*

Yes/No questions

Did I **bake** a cake?
Did he/she **play** with me?
Did it **pop** open?
Did you/we/they **cry** at
the end of the movie?

Affirmative answers

Yes, { I / he/she / it / you/we/they } did.

Negative answers

No, { I / he/she / it / you/we/they } didn't.

The simple past tense: information questions

Wh- word + *did* + subject + base form of verb

What	**did**	she	**bake**?
When	**did**	he	**dance**?
Where	**did**	they	**play**?
Why	**did**	they	**cry**?
How	**did**	they	**arrive** at the concert?
Who	**did**	you	**call** last night?

Answers

She **baked** some cookies.
He **danced** at the end of the night.
They **played** in the yard.
They **cried** because the movie was sad.
They **arrived** by taxi.
I **called** my brother.

Who + verb in simple past tense

Who **played** in the band?

Paula, Antonio, and Emily **played** in the band.

Practice

The simple past tense: regular verbs

Affirmative and negative statements

1 Complete the sentences with the simple past tense of the verbs.

1. You (*try*) ___tried___ to get the main part in our play.

2. Mateo (*like*) _____ the movie last night.

3. Jessica and I (*study*) _____ at the library.

4. The rabbits (*hop*) _____ around in our garden this morning.

5. A week ago, Anita (*borrow*) _____ my new blue sweater for the party.

6. I (*play*) _____ the piano for my class's concert last night.

7. She (*hug*) _____ me when she (*arrive*) _____ home.

8. Mom (*drop*) _____ me off at school yesterday.

2 Rewrite the sentences. Make the <u>underlined</u> simple past tense verbs negative. Use contractions when possible.

1. You <u>closed</u> the car windows last night.
   You didn't close the car windows last night.

2. My sister <u>mopped</u> the kitchen floor yesterday.
   _____

3. I <u>used</u> my new exercise bike this morning.
   _____

4. Matthew <u>practiced</u> basketball at the park after school yesterday.
   _____

5. Yoko and Linda <u>attended</u> our meeting a week ago.
   _____

6. Last month, Hiroshi, Luisa, and I <u>jogged</u> every morning before school.
   _____

7. My mother <u>worried</u> about me.
   _____

8. We <u>enjoyed</u> the party last weekend.
   _____

Yes/No questions

3 **Complete the questions using the cues.**

1. (*he / wash*) __Did he wash__ the car at the car wash?

2. (*Mom and Tanner / prepare*) _____ this chicken? It's delicious!

3. (*we / finish*) _____ the race on time?

4. (*I / return*) _____ your black jacket?

5. (*you / learn*) _____ those dances at school or at the dance club?

6. (*Jewel / sing*) _____ for an hour at her last concert?

7. (*it / rain*) _____ last night?

8. (*they / clean*) _____ their room this morning?

9. (*the red car / stop*) _____ at the stop sign?

4 **Complete the conversations using the cues. Use contractions when possible.**

1. A: Did Ramona and Janell go to the movies last night?

   B: No, __they didn't__. They (*study*) __studied__ for a test.

2. A: Did he walk to school this morning?

   B: Yes, _____.

3. A: Did you read a story to the first-graders?

   B: No, _____. I (*play*) _____ the piano for them.

4. A: Did I miss the first ten minutes of the show?

   B: Yes, _____.

5. A: Did it snow in Boston last week?

   B: No, _____. It (*rain*) _____.

6. A: Did Bessie like the school band?

   B: No, _____. She (*like*) _____ the school chorus.

7. A: Did we buy tomatoes at the supermarket?

   B: No, _____. We (*buy*) _____ some lettuce.

8. A: Did Domingo go to Clara's birthday party last weekend?

   B: Yes, _____.

9. A: Did you cook dinner?

   B: No, _____. I (*wash*) _____ the dishes.

The simple past tense: information questions with regular verbs

5 Unscramble the words to write questions. Then write the questions.

1. Paula / Lily / soccer / Where / play / did / yesterday / and
   Where did Paula and Lily play soccer yesterday?

2. dishes / wash / the / did / you / When
   _____

3. race / the / last / did / finish / in / Why / Rico
   _____

4. Mario / did / Who / hug
   _____

5. in / learn / she / English / class / her / did / What
   _____

6. When / borrow / I / dress / red / your / did
   _____

7. on / car / street / Why / we / did / park / the / that
   _____

8. picture / did / paint / How / they / that
   _____

6 Read the answers. Then write the questions using the underlined words as cues.

1. *Where did you and your parents travel to*
   last December?

   My parents and I traveled to <u>San Diego</u> last December.

2. _____

   James called <u>Carmen</u>.

3. _____

   I watched *Everybody Loves Raymond* <u>because it was very funny</u>.

4. _____

   My family and I celebrated my birthday <u>last Saturday night</u>.

5. _____

   Tina and Franklin <u>studied</u> after school.

6. _____

   Kenesha and Nicholas played at the <u>amusement park</u> yesterday afternoon.

7 Write information questions using your own ideas. Use the simple past tense and the question words below. In each question, use a past-time marker. Then write your answers to your questions.

1. Who _____
   _____

2. What _____
   _____

3. When _____
   _____

4. Where _____
   _____

5. Why _____
   _____

6. How _____
   _____

Unit 8

Grammar Highlights

The simple past tense: irregular verbs

Base form	Past tense	Base form	Past tense	Base form	Past tense
be	was, were	get	got	say	said
break	broke	give	gave	see	saw
bring	brought	go	went	sing	sang
buy	bought	have	had	sleep	slept
catch	caught	hear	heard	stand	stood
come	came	hurt	hurt	swim	swam
do	did	know	knew	take	took
drink	drank	lose	lost	teach	taught
drive	drove	make	made	tell	told
eat	ate	meet	met	think	thought
fall	fell	put	put		
fly	flew	run	ran		

Affirmative statements   Negative statements

I
He/She/It   } **heard** the noises.
We /You/They

I
He/She/It   } **did not/didn't** hear the noises.
We /You/They

I
He/She   } **was** at the park.
It

I
He/She   } **was not/wasn't** at the park.
It

We /You/They **were** at the park.

We /You/ They **were not/weren't** at the park.

Conjunctions: *and, but, so*

Use a conjunction and a comma to join two sentences.

Sara had a lead role, **and** *she was excellent.*

I tried to get there early, **but** *I arrived late.*

The show was a success, **so** *everyone celebrated.*

Remember: Conjunctions express different relationships.
And adds information.
But adds a contrast.
So expresses a result or effect.

Practice

The simple past tense: irregular verbs

1 Complete the sentences. Write the simple past tense of the irregular verbs in parentheses.

1. Alano (*bring*) __brought__ a fruit salad to the picnic.

2. Brittany and I (*catch*) _____ four fish at the lake.

3. Eartha (*hear*) _____ strange noises in the woods.

4. Vernon and Cara (*see*) _____ beautiful birds flying over the trees.

5. I (*tell*) _____ scary stories around the campfire at night.

6. You (*sing*) _____ songs for us after our dinner.

7. The baby bird (*fall*) _____ out of its nest in the tree.

2 Change the affirmative sentences into negative ones. Use contractions when possible.

1. They were in the auditorium by 2 P.M.
   They weren't in the auditorium by 2 P.M.

2. He got home from school before 3 P.M.
   _____

3. I did my homework after dinner.
   _____

4. My mom drove us to the baseball game last weekend.
   _____

5. You ate three chicken sandwiches!
   _____

6. She got an A on her math quiz.
   _____

7. Our dog lost its new toy.
   _____

8. My brother took my backpack to school.
   _____

9. We slept a lot over the weekend.
   _____

10. The new student in my class said *hello* to me.
    _____

11. Our neighbor's cat ran away last night.
    _____

12. She put the teapot on the stove.
    _____

13. We met Antonio and Elena at the movies.
    _____

14. My class made a collage of winter clothing fashions.
    _____

3 Write nine sentences about yourself using the simple past tense. Use the irregular verbs in this unit and the past-time markers in parentheses.

Examples:

Yesterday morning, I ate cereal for breakfast.

My sister and I swam in our neighbor's pool

last weekend.

1. (*yesterday morning*) _____
   _____

2. (*last weekend*) _____
   _____

3. (*a month ago*) _____
   _____

4. (*last night*) _____
   _____

5. (*yesterday afternoon*) _____
   _____

6. (*three days ago*) _____
   _____

7. (*last summer*) _____
   _____

8. (*a week ago*) _____
   _____

9. (*a few minutes ago*) _____
   _____

Conjunctions: *and, but, so*

4 Combine the sentences. Write *and, but,* or *so*. Use a comma before each conjunction.

1. Anita slept until 11 A.M. on Saturday. I got up at 7 A.M.
   Anita slept until 11 A.M. on Saturday, but I got
   up at 7 A.M.

2. Han-su caught five fish. His mother cooked them for dinner.
   _____
   _____

3. It started to rain. We left the park.
   _____
   _____

4. You went to the dance last night. I stayed home.
   _____
   _____

5. I rode my bike over a nail. It didn't get a flat tire.
   _____
   _____

6. She wants to get an A on her test. She is studying tonight.
   _____
   _____

7. She finished her dance. Then the audience applauded.
   _____
   _____

5 Combine the sentences. Write *and, but,* or *so*. Use a comma before each conjunction.

1. The Riveras cooked the Thanksgiving dinner. We brought the desserts.
   The Riveras cooked the Thanksgiving dinner,

   and we brought the desserts.

2. Clara and Jessica left the dance at 10 P.M. I left at 11 P.M.

   _____

   _____

3. It's raining. I'm going to take my umbrella.

   _____

   _____

4. You thought that the play was terrible. I agreed with you.

   _____

   _____

5. Andrew studied hard for the test. He got a 95.

   _____

   _____

6. Lee did a good job at work. She got a promotion.

   _____

   _____

7. I bought my sister a new dress. She didn't like it.

   _____

   _____

8. I wanted to go to the movies. I didn't feel well.

   _____

   _____

9. Michelle should return your bracelet. You won't get upset with her.

   _____

   _____

10. Latoya, Raul, and I really liked the movie. You liked the book better.

   _____

   _____

Unit 9

Grammar Highlights

Past Continuous

Affirmative Statements	**Negative Statements**
I/He/She/It **was running**.	I/He/She/It **was not (wasn't) running**.
You/We/They **were running**.	You/We/They **were not (weren't) running**.

When and *While*

I **was doing** my homework *when* Paula arrived.
While I **was doing** my homework, Paula arrived.

> **Remember:** Use *when* with the simple past. Use *while* with the past continuous.

The Simple Past Versus the Past Continuous

Simple Past	**Past Continuous**
I **cleaned** my room yesterday.	At eight o'clock last night I **was cleaning** my room.
Carol **worked** yesterday.	Carol **was working** between 9 A.M. and 5 P.M. yesterday.
We **studied** last night.	We **were studying** at nine o'clock last night.

> **Remember:** Use the simple past for a completed action in the past. Use the past continuous to express an action that was in progress at a particular time in the past.

Practice

Past Continuous; *When* and *While*

1 Complete the sentences with the past continuous form of the verbs in parentheses.

At seven o'clock last night . . .

1. I (*do*) __was doing__ my homework.
2. Mom (*make*) _____ dinner.
3. Carlos (*use*) _____ the computer.
4. Kate and Abby (*listen*) _____ to music.
5. it (*rain*) _____.
6. Dan (*fix*) _____ the camera.
7. the neighbors (*have*) _____ a party.
8. you (*try*) _____ to study.

2 Rewrite the sentences from Exercise 1 in the negative.

At seven o'clock last night . . .

1. _I wasn't doing my homework._
2. _____
3. _____
4. _____
5. _____
6. _____
7. _____
8. _____

3 Circle the correct word in each sentence.

1. I was trying to call you (*when* / *while*) the bus arrived.
2. Kathy fell (*when* / *while*) she was carrying a cake.
3. Yoko's tooth fell out (*when* / *while*) she was eating chocolate.
4. (*When* / *While*) you called me last night, I was talking to John.
5. (*When* / *While*) Tania was fixing the computer, her brother watched her.
6. (*When* / *While*) the teacher arrived in class, the students were preparing a surprise party for her birthday.

4 Write sentences in the past continuous tense using the cues.

1. Bill / talk to Martha (*yes*)
   Bill was talking to Martha.
2. we / swim / in the river (*no*)
   We weren't swimming in the river.
3. Mom / make breakfast (*no*)
   _____
4. the children / play in class (*yes*)
   _____
5. you / clean your room (*yes*)
   _____
6. I / sleep in the car (*no*)
   _____
7. the dog / bark all night (*yes*)
   _____
8. Tom and I / do homework together (*no*)
   _____

Practice

Simple Past Versus Past Continuous; *When* and *While*

5 Circle the correct form of the verbs so that one clause is in the simple past and the other is in the past continuous.

1. I (*met* / *was meeting*) Pat while I (*walked* / *was walking*) to the park.

2. Helen (*read* / *was reading*) when she (*fell* / *was falling*) asleep.

3. She (*wore* / *was wearing*) a red dress when I (*saw* / *was seeing*) her.

4. While we (*danced* / *were dancing*), I (*stepped* / *was stepping*) on his feet.

5. They (*used* / *were using*) the computer when the storm (*started* / *was starting*).

6. While we (*talked* / *were talking*), a car (*came by* / *was coming by*) very fast.

7. The cat (*jumped* / *was jumping*) on the dog while he (*slept* / *was sleeping*).

8. He (*thought* / *was thinking*) about Meg when she (*called* / *was calling*).

9. Omar (*swam* / *was swimming*) in the lake when he (*saw* / *was seeing*) the boat.

10. A bird (*flew* / *was flying*) into the house while the kids (*sat* / *were sitting*) in the kitchen.

6 Write the simple past or the past continuous form of the verbs.

1. Graciela (*fall*) _____fell_____ while she (*ride*) __was riding__ her bicycle.

2. He (*walk*) _____ to his car when he (*lose*) _____ his wallet.

3. I turned the volume down because you (*do*) _____ your homework.

4. They (*buy*) _____ a house a year ago.

5. He (*meet*) _____ his girlfriend while he (*work*) _____ at the library.

6. Debbie (*jog*) _____ in the park when she (*find*) _____ the necklace.

7. While she (*use*) _____ the computer, it (*crash*) _____.

8. We (*have*) _____ a party when my parents (*arrive*) _____.

9. I (*watch*) _____ my favorite show when you (*call*) _____.

10. Brian (*talk*) _____ on the phone when his girlfriend (*come over*) _____.

Practice

1 Complete the sentences. Circle *when* or *while*.

1. (*When* / *While*) Lily was sitting on the ground, she saw a snake.
2. Marie was riding her bike (*when* / *while*) I yelled at her.
3. We were walking to school (*when* / *while*) we saw an accident.
4. Mom's cell phone rang (*when* / *while*) she was driving home.
5. Tony was making lunch (*when* / *while*) he cut his finger.
6. (*When* / *While*) Jack was using the computer, the lights went out.
7. (*While* / *When*) I came home from school, my sister was crying.
8. Jill broke a plate (*when* / *while*) she was washing the dishes.
9. Greg was playing video games (*while* / *when*) his dad arrived.

8 Complete the sentences using the cues.

When Ana arrived at the party . . .

1. Ben / talk / to Michael
   Ben was talking to Michael.

2. Isabella / drink / a soda
   _____

3. Dave and Maria / dance
   _____

4. Lily and Oscar / laugh
   _____

5. Dan / eat / a sandwich
   _____

6. a few students / sit / on the floor
   _____

While Ana was talking to Isabella . . .

7. Kenji / open the window
   Kenji opened the window.

8. Martina and Lucy / go / into the kitchen
   _____

9. Yumiko / take / a photograph
   _____

10. the lights / go out / in the room
    _____

11. everybody / start / to sing / "Happy Birthday"
    _____

Unit 10

Grammar Highlights

Making Comparisons with Adjectives

Positive	Comparative	Superlative
old	old**er than**	**the** old**est**
hot	hot**ter than**	**the** hot**test**
pretty	prett**ier than**	**the** prett**iest**
famous	**more** famous **than**	**the most** famous
difficult	**more** difficult **than**	**the most** difficult
interesting	**more** interesting **than**	**the most** interesting

Remember: Use the comparative to compare two people, things, or places. My brother is **older than** my sister.

Remember: Use the superlative to compare three or more people, things, or places. Alberto is **the fastest** runner on the track team.

Remember: Here are some rules for forming the comparative and superlative forms:
- For most one-syllable adjectives, add -er or -est. hard — hard**er** — hard**est**
- For one-syllable adjectives that end in a vowel and a consonant, double the consonant and add -er or -est. big — big**ger** — big**gest**
- For adjectives that end in -y, change the -y to -i and add -er or -est. funny — funn**ier** — funn**iest**
- To form the comparative form of some two-syllable adjectives and adjectives with three or more syllables, use **more . . . than**. To form the superlative form, use **the most . . . .** Roller-skating is **more** exciting **than** swimming. Skiing is **the most** exciting sport of all.

Comparative and Superlative of Irregular Adjectives

Positive	Comparative	Superlative
good	**better than**	**the best**
bad	**worse than**	**the worst**
far	far**ther than**	**the** far**thest**

as + adjective + as

Your hair is **as curly as** mine.
His house is **as big as** yours.

Remember: Use *as* + adjective + *as* to express equality.

Practice

Making Comparisons with Adjectives

1 Complete the sentences. Write the comparative form of the adjectives.

1. Lauren is (*short*) _shorter than_ Matthew.
2. The movie is (*funny*) _____ the book.
3. My English class is (*easy*) _____ my math class this year.
4. The computer table is (*big*) _____ the TV table.
5. My younger sister is (*lazy*) _____ I am.
6. My father is (*old*) _____ my mother.
7. My friend Lucas is (*tall*) _____ you are.
8. Dolores is (*popular*) _____ Nicole.
9. Going to the amusement park is (*exciting*) _____ going to the city park.
10. The necklace is (*expensive*) _____ the bracelet.

2 Write sentences comparing the people, things, or places. Use the cues and the comparative form of the adjectives in parentheses.

1. my car / your car / (*small*)
   My car is smaller than your car.

2. my book / your book / (*interesting*)
   My book is more interesting than your book.

3. a runner / a jogger / (*fast*)
   _____

4. that suitcase / my backpack / (*large*)
   _____

5. Su-Mi / Elena / (*short*)
   _____

6. studying for my test / going to the movies / (*important*)
   _____

7. a Chevrolet / a Ferrari / (*cheap*)
   _____

8. the cheese slices / the turkey slices / (*thin*)
   _____

9. these oranges / those apples / (*sweet*)
   _____

10. the ruler / the pen / (*long*)
    _____

11. today's homework / yesterday's homework / (*difficult*)
    _____

12. Orlando, Florida / New York City / (*hot*)
    _____

Practice

3 Write sentences comparing the items. Use the cues and an adjective of your choice.

1. a baseball / a soccer ball
   A baseball is smaller than
   a soccer ball.

2. rock and roll / jazz
   _____
   _____

3. writing English / reading English
   _____
   _____

4. a car / a truck
   _____
   _____

5. a cheeseburger / a cheese sandwich
   _____
   _____

6. Colombia / Costa Rica
   _____
   _____

7. a dog / a cat
   _____
   _____

8. the weather today / the weather yesterday
   _____
   _____

9. (one TV show) / (another TV show)
   _____
   _____

10. (one music group) / (another music group)
    _____
    _____

4 Complete the sentences. Write the superlative form of the adjectives.

1. Paco is (fast) _the fastest_ swimmer on our team.

2. Our last vacation was (relaxing) _____ vacation of all.

3. This box is (heavy) _____ box of all.

4. My sister Janet is (slow) _____ eater in my family.

5. Salad is (healthy) _____ item on the menu.

6. This video game is (exciting) _____ game to play.

7. The red chair is (comfortable) _____ chair in our house.

8. Our blanket is (soft) _____ blanket of all.

5 Write sentences using the comparative form of the adjectives.

1. (nervous) _Before a math test, I'm more nervous_ _than you are._

2. (quiet) _____
   _____

3. (beautiful) _____
   _____

4. (dirty) _____
   _____

5. (hot) _____
   _____

6. (dangerous) _____
   _____

Practice

6 Look at the pictures. Then complete the sentences. Write the comparative or superlative form of the adjective.

1. The car is _____big_____.
2. The van is _____ the car.
3. The truck is _____ of all.

4. The necklace is _____cheap_____.
5. The bracelet is _____ the necklace.
6. The earrings are _____ of all.

7. Elena was _____lucky_____.
8. Odessa was _____ Elena.
9. Brittany was _____ of all.

Comparative and Superlative of Irregular Adjectives

7 Write the comparative or the superlative form of the adjectives.

1. Your video camera is (*good*) ___better than___ Roland's.

2. Keiko's apartment is (*far*) _____ my house.
3. Lisa's apartment is (*far*) _____ of all.
4. Pedro's handwriting is (*bad*) _____ yours.
5. My handwriting is (*bad*) _____ of all.
6. That amusement park is (*large*) _____ of all.
7. A chicken sandwich is (*good*) _____ a cheeseburger.
8. A big salad is (*good*) _____ of all the meals.

as + adjective + as

8 Write sentences using the cues and *as* + adjective + *as*.

1. Tina / Rosa / tall
   Tina is as tall as Rosa.

2. *Spider-man* / *The Lion King* / exciting
   _____

3. the movie / the book / scary
   _____

4. Picasso / Monet / famous
   _____

5. Mel Gibson / Tom Cruise / handsome
   _____

9 Write sentences with *as* + adjective + *as*. Use your own ideas.

Example: *Skateboarding is as exciting as surfing.*

1. _____
2. _____
3. _____
4. _____
5. _____

Unit 11

Grammar Highlights

Should/Shouldn't

Affirmative statements

I
You
He/She } **should take** some aspirin.
We
They

Negative statements

I
You
He/She } **shouldn't watch** too much TV.
We
They

Yes/No questions

Should I **take** an aspirin?

Short answers

Yes, you **should**. / No, you **shouldn't**.

> **Remember:** Use *should* to give advice.

> **Remember:** The base form of the verb follows *should*. The negative form of *should* is *should not* (*shouldn't*). *Should* is the same for all persons (*I, you, he, she, it, we,* and *they*).

Habitual Past: *Used to*

Affirmative statements

I **used to get up** early. I don't anymore.
Anna **used to travel** a lot.

Negative statements

He **didn't use to exercise**, but now he does.
We **didn't use to have** dogs.

Yes/No questions

Did you **use to get up** early?

Short answers

Yes, I **did**. / No, I **didn't**.

> **Remember:** *Used to* expresses past habits or situations that no longer exist in the present.

> **Remember:** The base form of the verb follows *used to.*

Practice

Should/Shouldn't

Affirmative and Negative Statements

1 Complete the sentences with *should* or *shouldn't*.

1. Ben is sleeping. You _shouldn't_ make noise.

2. Kate's room is messy. She _____ clean it.

3. Carlos lost my new CD. He _____ buy me a new one.

4. People _____ drive too fast. It's very dangerous.

5. They stayed up all night. They _____ go home and rest.

6. My back hurts. I _____ lift that heavy box.

7. The cats are hungry. We _____ feed them dinner.

8. It's midnight. You _____ call your friend's house now.

9. A big storm is coming. We _____ use the computer.

10. It's very hot today. You _____ stay inside their cool house.

2 Complete the sentences with the words from the box.

should see	should send
shouldn't eat	should exercise
shouldn't stay up	should take
shouldn't go out	should sleep
shouldn't wear	should get

1. Mario's hair is too long.

   He _should get_ a haircut.

2. We're going to have a test tomorrow.

   We _____ too late.

3. It's very cold outside.

   You _____ without your coat.

4. Olga wants to lose weight.

   She _____ at the gym.

5. Peter's parents work a lot.

   They _____ a vacation.

6. We saw the new Spielberg movie. It was great.

   You _____ it, too.

7. He's very tired these days.

   He _____ more.

8. The children's teeth hurt.

   They _____ candy.

9. Tom's birthday is next week.

   We _____ him a card.

10. It's cold today.

    You _____ shorts.

Practice

3 Read each situation. Then complete the advice. Write *should* or *shouldn't* and an appropriate verb for each sentence.

1. Mario has a bad headache.

   He ___*should take*___ an aspirin.

2. Your mother has a sore throat.

   She _____ to the doctor.

3. Paulo is always tired.

   He _____ to bed earlier.

4. Meg and Jane are always late for school.

   They _____ earlier.

5. You have a test tomorrow.

   You _____ to the movies tonight.

6. Your father can't sleep at night.

   He _____ too much coffee.

7. Your brother's back is hurting him.

   He _____ that heavy suitcase.

8. The girls are outside in the hot sun.

   They _____ hats and sunglasses.

Yes/No questions

4 Read the answers. Then write questions with *should.*

1. *Should I take some aspirin?* _____

   No. You shouldn't take aspirin. You should call a doctor.

2. _____

   Yes. You should memorize the grammar rules.

3. _____

   No. We shouldn't sit in the first row.

4. _____

   No. Joe shouldn't try to fix the car. Last time he ruined it.

5. _____

   Yes. We should return the books to the library.

6. _____

   Yes. You should wait for me in the car.

Practice

Habitual Past: *Used to*

Affirmative and negative statements

5 Write sentences with *used to* or *didn't use to*. Use the cues.

1. Kim and Tom / go to the movies a lot (✓)
   Kim and Tom used to go to the movies a lot.

2. Kim / pay all the time (✗)
   Kim didn't use to pay all the time.

3. we / watch a lot of TV after school (✓)
   _____

4. my family and I /live in a big city (✗)
   _____

5. they / read teen magazines (✗)
   _____

6. my parents / travel abroad often (✓)
   _____

7. Frank and Juan/ go to the movies (✓)
   _____

8. I / play a lot of video games (✗)
   _____

9. Martha / go to the gym (✓)
   _____

10. Tran / live in New York (✓)
    _____

6 Complete the sentences about yourself.

1. When I was younger, I used to _____
   _____.

2. I didn't use to _____
   when I was younger.

Yes/No questions

7 Look at the picture. Then write questions with *used to* and short answers. Use the cues in the box.

~~have long hair~~	collect rocks
have curly hair	be chubby
wear eyeglasses	have a cat
ride a motorcycle	

Paulo (before)

Paulo (now)

1. *Did Paulo used to have long hair?*
   Yes, he did.

2. _____
   _____

3. _____
   _____

4. _____
   _____

5. _____
   _____

6. _____
   _____

7. _____

Unit 12

Grammar Highlights

Future Tense: *Will*

Affirmative statements

I **will go** home after class.

We **will have** a party soon.

She **will come** later.

Negative statements

I **will not (won't) go** home after class.

We **will not (won't) have** a party soon.

He **will not (won't) come** later.

> **Remember:**
> • The base form of the verb follows *will*.
> • The contractions of pronouns and *will* are: *I'll, you'll, he'll, she'll, it'll, we'll,* and *they'll*.

Yes/No questions

Will you **be** home tomorrow?
Will she **be** here for the test?

Short answers

Yes, I **will**.
No, she **won't**.

> **Remember:**
> • *Will* is not contracted with the personal pronouns in short *yes* answers.
> • Will you buy a new CD? Yes, I **will**. (Not: Yes, I'll.)
> • Will Anna come tomorrow? Yes, she **will**. (Not: Yes, she'll.)
> • The contraction for *will not* is *won't*.

May and *Might*

Affirmative statements

It **may rain** tomorrow.
They **may watch** TV after dinner.

It **might rain** tomorrow.
They **might watch** TV after dinner.

Negative statements

It **may not rain** tomorrow.
They **may not watch** TV after dinner.

It **might not rain** tomorrow.
They **might not watch** TV after dinner.

> **Remember:** Do not use a contraction for *may not* and *might not*.

> **Remember:** *May/might* + the base form of the verb expresses possibility. *Might* has the same meaning as *may*. *Will* expresses something that is sure to happen.

Practice

Future Tense with *Will*

1 Complete the sentences with *will* or *won't*. Use the contracted form of *will* with a pronoun whenever possible.

My name's Chico.

I ___'ll___ finish
    (1)

high school next

year. My friends

_____ go to college, but I _____ go
(2)   (3)

right away. My girlfriend Maria and I

_____ take a year off. She _____
(4)   (5)

get a job, and I _____ get a job, too.
             (6)

We _____ work for a while and save
    (7)

money. Then I _____ travel and visit my
         (8)

cousins in Mexico. They _____ show me
           (9)

around. We _____ go to the beach for
      (10)

sure. I hope the weather _____ be nice
         (11)

and sunny. Unfortunately, there _____ be
        (12)

enough time to visit everything. When I get

back, I _____ think about college. I hope
    (13)

I _____ be able to find a college that
  (14)

offers computer programming. After college,

I _____ find a job. Maria and I _____
  (15)   (16)

get married until we finish college, get jobs,

and save some money.

2 Unscramble the words to write *Yes/No* questions about the text in Exercise 1. Then write short answers using the cues.

1. Chico / finish / this year / Will / high school / ?

   Will Chico finish high school this year?

   No, *he won't.*

2. high school / take / Maria / Will / a year off / after / ?

   _____

   Yes, _____.

3. jobs / Will / get / they / ?

   _____

   Yes, _____.

4. to / Chico / travel / Will / Mexico / ?

   _____

   Yes, _____.

5. Chico / Will / Maria / with / travel / ?

   _____

   No, _____.

6. enough time / Chico / have / Will / everything / to visit / ?

   _____

   No, _____.

7. Chico / Will / and / get married / Maria / jobs / before / get / they / ?

   _____

   No, _____.

Practice

3 Complete the sentences. Use *will* and a verb from the box. Use each verb only once. Use the contracted form of *will* with a pronoun whenever possible.

start	keep	~~have~~	visit
get	win	meet	become

Many Adventures

1. You *'ll have* _____ many adventures.
2. Sarah _____ a new boyfriend.
3. You _____ an A in English.
4. Your friends _____ you in Argentina.
5. Yumiko _____ the lottery.
6. Carl _____ a famous movie director.
7. Elena _____ her friend's secret.
8. The math test _____ at eight o'clock.

4 Write *Yes/No* questions for the sentences in Exercise 3. Then write short answers. Be sure to give both negative and affirmative answers.

1. A: *Will I have many adventures?*
   B: *Yes, you will.*
2. A: *Will Sarah meet a new boyfriend?*
   B: *No, she won't.*
3. A: _____
   B: _____
4. A: _____
   B: _____
5. A: _____
   B: _____
6. A: _____
   B: _____
7. A: _____
   B: _____
8. A: _____
   B: _____

May and *Might*

5 Complete the sentences. Circle the correct words.

1. A: Where are the children?
   B: I don't know. They ((may) / will) be outside.
2. A: This backpack is heavy.
   B: I (*might / will*) carry it for you.
3. A: Is Oscar coming to the party?
   B: I'm not sure. He (*may / will*) stay home.
4. A: What are your plans for the summer?
   B: I don't have any plans. I (*might / will*) find a job.
5. A: Can I have my 'NSync CDs back?
   B: Sure. I (*may / will*) return them tonight.
6. A: Do you think it will snow tomorrow?
   B: I don't know. It (*may / will*), or it (*may not / will not*).

Practice

6 Complete the conversation with *will* or *may/might*. Use the contracted form of *will* with a pronoun whenever possible.

Kim: _____Will_____ Tom go surfing with us?
(1)

Michael: Yes, he _____will_____. He _____'ll_____
(2)   (3)
meet us in the morning.

Kim: _____ he bring his new
(4)
surfboard?

Michael: Of course, he _____ bring his
(5)
new surfboard!

Kim: _____ Alicia come with us, too?
(6)

Michael: I don't know. She wasn't feeling well
last night, so she _____not come.
(7)
I _____ call her later, anyway.
(8)

Kim: Should we take sandwiches with us?

Michael: I think we should. There is one nice
restaurant near the beach, but it
_____ not be open tomorrow.
(9)
You never know.

Kim: _____ the weather be nice?
(10)

Michael: Yes. They said it _____ be hot
(11)
and sunny.

Kim: Great! I _____ see you tomorrow.
(12)

7 Look at the chart about Dan's, Ann's, and Sue's summer plans. Write sentences with *will, won't, may/might,* and *may not/might not.*

	Dan	Ann and Sue
Go to the beach	✓	?
Travel to Mexico	?	✗
Read some books	✗	✓

✓ = yes   ✗ = no   ? = possibly

1. _Dan will go to the beach._
2. _Ann and Sue may not go to the beach._
3. _____
4. _____
5. _____
6. _____

8 Write six sentences about the coming weekend. In Sentences 1 and 2, tell what you *will* do this weekend. In sentences 3 and 4, tell what you *won't* do this weekend. In sentences 5 and 6, tell what you *might* do this weekend.

1. _____
2. _____
3. _____
4. _____
5. _____
6. _____